In *A New Parish Guide to Grief Ministry* Anne Marie Mahoney provides gentle guidance for those who walk the long and lonely path of grief. With sensitivity and grace, she provides practical ideas for structuring a support system that helps those grieving the deaths of loved ones. Each session draws upon the lived experience of those in various stages of the bereavement process and offers creative ways for them to give expression to their sadness as well as their hope.

■ **KATHY HENDRICKS**, *Acquisitions Editor, Twenty-Third Publications*

This thoughtful and elegant eight-session guide to running a creative bereavement program fits perfect in that window of time after our loved one has died, but before we can truly contemplate our new normal. Rich with opportunity to process and integrate grief through art, Scripture, and education, this guide helps those who might feel less confident in leading a group, but aware of a need. All the tools are right here, along with the author's warm and supportive tone and clear lay out of the program. I would happily put this guide into the hands of a compassionate soul looking to help those who have suffered a loss.

■ **SAIREY LUTERMAN**, *Certified Thanatologist, Lexington, MA*

This all-inclusive guide offers a sensibly arranged progression of themes and gatherings for leading participants to face grief and grow through it. The handbook's eight meetings can be adapted to fit different situations, needs, and preferences. Its proposed presentations, discussions, and activities are well grounded in fifteen wise principles, brought to expression through a marvelous array of musical, visual, and literary resources. This creative approach makes the compendium quite distinctive. Anne Marie Mahoney draws on her own story to invite leaders and attendees to reflect on their own. She offers no shortcut through grief, but lays out pathways toward insight and peace. The book is rich in tips gleaned from the author's own experiences of dealing with loss and of delicately leading sessions for others.

■ **FATHER GEORGE EVANS**, *Pastor, Holy Name Parish, West Roxbury, MA*

Anne Marie Mahoney's *A New Parish Guide to Grief Ministry* is a clear and competent handbook for establishing or for improving bereavement ministry. Grounded in her personal experience of grief and facilitating bereavement groups, she offers a fresh, creative, well-organized template for bereavement groups that can be easily adapted to the needs of the participants. Her warm, inviting style blends professional knowledge, practical wisdom, and organizational expertise into a presentation that will truly touch the hearts of readers.

■ REV. MSGR. JAMES A. MONGELLUZZO, STD, *Professor of Liturgical Studies and Homiletics, Pope St. John XXIII National Seminary, Weston, MA*

Ecclesial ministers who have the privilege to accompany those who mourn will find here a resource that will be an instrument of hope. A joy to use as they create a safe space, a place of hospitality, a place where peace will come "dropping slow" for those whose hearts are broken, who are trying to recover from life-altering changes.

■ SUSAN J. KAY, *Facilitator Boston College School of Theology and Ministry, Crossroads Program*

A NEW PARISH GUIDE TO GRIEF MINISTRY

A New Parish Guide to
GRIEF MINISTRY

Creative Ways to Implement a Program
of **HEALING** and **GROWTH**

ANNE MARIE S. MAHONEY

**TWENTY-THIRD
PUBLICATIONS**
twentythirdpublications.com

Twenty-Third Publications
977 Hartford Turnpike Unit A; Waterford, CT 06385
(860) 437-3012 or (800) 321-0411; www.twentythirdpublications.com

ISBN: 978-1-62785-775-8
Printed in the U.S.A.

 A division of Bayard, Inc.

For Brian,

who made everything possible,

who always believed in me,

who is with me every day.

CONTENTS

Acknowledgments

I offer heartfelt thanks to my Boston College profes-
sors, my friends and colleagues in ministry, the Beech
Street Senior Center in Belmont, Massachusetts, the
Merry Widows, who started me on this path, and my
friends for their patient listening, without whom this
book would not have come to fruition.

Special thanks to Erika for PTSD information, Debi
for taking my headshot, and Kathy Hendricks for con-
necting me to Twenty-Third Publications, making this
book possible.

More than anything, loving thanks to my children and
Scout the literary cat who helped me get this book
finished!

INTRODUCTION

Someone I loved once gave me
a box full of darkness.

It took me years to understand
that this, too, was a gift.

[MARY OLIVER, *THE USES OF SORROW*]

Sometime after my husband, Brian, died, I reflected on all that had transpired and realized that I hardly knew myself. Whoever or whatever I was before he became ill was not who I was at that juncture, nor is it who I am today. And therein lies the story. Grieving is ultimately about a story and how one allows it to unfold, page by page. Grieving is painful and lonely and hard. Grieving is being lost in a box full of darkness. Grieving is a long journey with no GPS and only a vague idea of where the destination might be. How do we get there? What tools do we need to climb out of the darkness? I hope this "Creative Bereavement" program is at least the gift of a flashlight and a map for the grievers in your community.

You sleepwalk through that first year following the death of a loved one, doing what must be done in the moment and hoping for the best. One day, about a year after the death, you wake up and ask yourself, with real awe, "What just happened?" That is the moment the grieving begins in earnest. The paperwork is done, relatives have gone back to their routines, and friends have stopped asking how you are doing. You feel alone, not quite sure who you are anymore, and you do not see any ready support or relief. You are lost in "the box full of darkness." I needed comfort and there was nowhere to turn.

Sixteen months after my husband died, his brother died of a similar illness. His daughter who had cared for him called me the afternoon following his death. She was chaperoning her son's class trip to a museum. Sitting on a bench while the kids ate lunch, she reached out just to talk. She vented about her father's death, her struggle to meet his needs, the waves of emotions rushing over her. She was feeling overwhelmed with grief and responsibilities. I had been caught in those same waves, which sometimes felt like riptides. I mostly listened. Her feelings and questions were so familiar. This sparked an idea about offering others an opportunity to "come cry with me."

Meanwhile, in the year following Brian's death, the spouses of four friends died as well. We banded together, dubbed ourselves "The Merry Widows," and gathered for pot-luck dinners every few months. At first, we shared information about life insurance, financial planning, and headstones. That morphed into mutual support over struggling children, annoying in-laws, selling a business and a house. As the drama settled, we spent long hours exploring the deeply personal experiences of being youngish widows. Saving his tools and fishing gear. Leaving his hat and keys on the table by the front door. Keeping his favorite ties on the valet in the bedroom. Holding on and letting go. And what gave us comfort—his favorite song, his favorite meal, his favorite sweater.

Busy lives, pressing responsibilities, well-meaning friends and family all work to deny us the unfettered opportunity to grieve. By the time we hit that first-year milestone, seemingly everyone wants us to "get over it" and "move on" or "get a new life." The Merry Widows helped each other. Where, I wondered, do others turn for support? Where is the guidebook that shows others how to grieve effectively?

I remembered that I would be moved to tears by a jewelry store commercial that played "I Got You Babe" in the background. It was one of "our" songs. When Lady Mary railed against her Downton Abbey family over the sudden death of her husband, I cheered. I had been there. I was mesmerized by an episode of the television show *Bones* that portrayed an Army Ranger who had lost one of his soldiers. So close to Brian's Vietnam experience. These were all triggers for my story. There was something powerful in my emotional response to these media experiences. I found each encounter uniquely healing.

With all these pieces floating in my head, a program began to gel as I started to explore how I got through the first couple of years following my husband's death using touchstones in the arts—and how others might do so as well. As a parish pastoral minister, I had the knowledge and experience to incorporate the arts into a bereavement program. I found that the programs available elsewhere were not adequately meeting the long-term needs of grievers. Slowly, I formed "Creative Bereavement" by gathering all the tears and pain along with the laughter and joy to give others some insights into picking up the threads of their own stories and moving forward after the death of a loved one.

This book is the result of my work, one of the gifts I discovered deep in the box full of darkness. I combine my own experience of both grief and education in grief and loss along with what I have learned from the groups I facilitated. This program can serve as a template for your own program. Use what works for you. Make it your own.

The book is divided into two parts. The first part offers basic information on grief and loss, leading a bereavement group, and hints about setting up and running the program. The second part contains the actual session details. Use these as an outline or a script. Rearrange the topics to suit your group. Bring in your own songs, Scripture, articles, or favorite video clips. Incorporate movement according to your group's comfort level. Know your participants and choose materials accordingly. The program should reflect what is meaningful to your group. The bibliography contains the sources from which I gathered material.

I hope you find the information useful and the program healing. May your grievers find their gift in their box full of darkness.

PART 1
Background

1

Why a "Creative Bereavement" Program?

Then the word of the LORD came to him, saying, "What are you doing here, Elijah?" He answered,..."I alone am left...."

He said, "Go out and stand on the mountain before the LORD, for the LORD is about to pass by." Now there was a great wind, so strong that it was splitting mountains and breaking rocks in pieces before the LORD, but the LORD was not in the wind; and after the wind an earthquake, but the LORD was not in the earthquake; and after the earthquake a fire, but the LORD was not in the fire; and after the fire a sound of sheer silence. When Elijah heard it, he wrapped his face in his mantle and went out and stood at the entrance of the cave. Then there came a voice to him that said, "What are you doing here, Elijah?"

[1 KINGS 19:9B, 10B, 11–13]

I remember my first Elijah experience. Brian's funeral was on a Friday. On Saturday, the house was empty after my children and siblings returned to their respective homes. I was utterly alone and completely numb. I ate leftovers from the funeral luncheon and choked on the fragrance of the funeral flowers that filled my house. I understood in a visceral way why my mother hated gladioli. That afternoon I walked to my parish, a little early for the weekend Mass. I sat near my usual spot, crunching myself against one of the pillars, almost trying to hide beside its solid bulk. I felt like Elijah wrapping his face in his mantle. As people began to fill the church, a few came to offer their condolences. My thin smile was automatic. Yes, I was fine. Thank you.

Eventually, the pastor approached me and, leaning in from the side aisle, asked, a bit annoyed, "What are you doing here?"

I was too stunned to answer. Reeling from the weeks of the wind, the earthquake, and the fire, I expected something more pastoral, such as "How are you doing?" or "Is anyone still at home with you?" or maybe "What can we do for you?" I didn't expect "What are you doing here?" followed by "You know we are going to pray for Brian today in the intentions. Maybe you don't want to hear that."

I could not fathom what was transpiring. I had lived in the parish since I was a child, as had Brian. This was supposed to be the place of comfort. This should be the cave where I could hide and wait for the sheer silence. Yes, I wanted to hear his name. I wanted the parish to acknowledge his death and his loss to the faith community. That church represented three generations of sacraments and commitment for both our extended families. Instead of the support and care I craved in this most vulnerable moment, I received a challenge: "What are you doing here?"

Forming the Program

In time, "What are you doing here?" became a theme for me. It is a pivotal question for grievers. As I started to work with the bereaved, I heard stories about relatives, friends, workplaces, places of worship, and community groups that could not meet the needs of those suffering a loss. It takes years for grievers to answer the question "What are you doing here?" Meanwhile, where do they find the special place that understands the question and the search for an answer?

As time passed, I became driven by the idea that if I did not feel supported, others might feel even more alienated. A neighboring parish offered an eight-week bereavement support group, which I attended. It was lovely but left me feeling empty. At each session, I kept thinking about songs and artwork and poems that would have fit so well with the facilitator's themes. The Scripture passages were well chosen, and questions were on point, but I wanted more. I almost brought the Alison Krauss song "Get Me Through December" to the session the week before Christmas. It seemed perfect, but I did not want to overstep. I became convinced that a bereavement program that included music, film clips, and poetry would be helpful for grievers.

Parishes, for the most part, meet the immediate needs of the bereaved with the wake/visitation and the funeral/memorial Mass, followed by a reception. However, when the casket has been lowered into the ground and the last luncheon dish is washed and put away, the bereavement team's involvement ends. They are not present for that long road of grief when their parishioner starts to focus on the uncertain future.

In planning my program, I posed two questions:

1. What would be the focus of my bereavement program?

2. How should I use the creative arts in my program?

Simply put: Why bereavement? Why creative? There are many good bereavement programs out there, and grievers should take advantage of them. However, many take place in clinical settings that don't address the spiritual aspect of bereavement. Others are in spiritual settings that may emphasize faith over coping. I am not a counselor, social worker, or psychologist. I am an educator. As a former high school English teacher and a parish pastoral associate and director of religious education, I was accustomed to weaving music, art, film, and poetry into the sacrament workshops I gave.

> **"Creative Bereavement" is designed to provide ongoing compassionate witness to grievers. Not just in the week following the death but for weeks and months and years after the loss.**

I wanted a program that was not clinical but pastoral—one that offered tools beyond the clinical as well as the spiritual.

"Creative Bereavement" is designed to provide ongoing compassionate witness to grievers. Not just in the week following the death but for weeks and months and years after the loss. Grievers often find the second year after the death to be the hardest. The paperwork is done; the legal requirements have been fulfilled; family, friends, and coworkers expect you to be "normal," but the reality of the loss is just setting in. Mine would be a what-comes-next program, a set of tools for both processing grief and moving forward with hope. A program that would encourage grievers to answer the question "What are you doing here?"

I believed that the creative arts could be a vehicle for exploring grief and loss, a key to productive grieving by teaching grievers how to express themselves in a way that is life-giving, is soothing, and forms a path to the future. Participants did not need any particular talent: they just should be able to remember a song; choose an image; listen to a poem, Scripture citation, or story; watch a video clip. And be open to finding a message or a memory of their loved one within a safe space for exploring their deepest yearnings.

The first program I ran was four weeks, with four themes, and was well received by a dozen women. I expanded to six-week and then eight-week programs and eventually ran half-day retreats and single sessions on grief and loss. My participants taught me so much that improved the program. Death could be represented by a kaleidoscope of origami strips. Comfort could come from a quilt made from a spouse's work shirts. Flute music could trigger soothing memories of a mother. Participants could find peace in watching the movies from which I showed clips.

My intuition that the arts could engage grievers and address their grief was confirmed with each new program. The evaluations participants gave me helped me to better meet their needs. We became partners in forming this program, in finding the gift.

2

The Program
and How It Works

I will arise and go now, and go to Innisfree,
And a small cabin build there, of clay and wattles made:
Nine bean-rows will I have there, a hive for the honey-bee,
And live alone in the bee-loud glade.

And I shall have some peace there, for peace comes dropping slow,
Dropping from the veils of the morning to where the cricket sings;
There midnight's all a glimmer, and noon a purple glow,
And evening full of the linnet's wings.

I will arise and go now, for always night and day
I hear lake water lapping with low sounds by the shore;
While I stand on the roadway, or on the pavements grey,
I hear it in the deep heart's core.

[WILLIAM BUTLER YEATS, "THE LAKE ISLE OF INNISFREE"]

When I was starting to develop my "Creative Bereavement" program, I attended the funeral of a former neighbor. At the end of the Mass, his daughter stood to deliver the words of remembrance. I expected a thoughtful eulogy for a beloved gentleman. She rose with a smile, stepped to the ambo, and explained that her father's favorite poem was William Butler Yeats' "The Lake Isle of Innisfree." She read the poem and sat down. I was surprised and disappointed. Then I went home and reread it, line by line. I realized how much wisdom it held about death and grief. Yeats, an early-twentieth-century Irish poet, was known for his belief in the "thin space" between life and death, between the present and the hereafter, between our perception and awareness of the continuing presence of our deceased loved ones.

"And I shall have some peace there, for peace comes dropping slow..." Grievers are looking for that peace. The drop-by-drop peace of understanding that our loved one is gone but remains with us in spirit, in memory, in love, in the thin space between night and day where we hear them in our deep heart's core. And so, in my program I try to respect the line between teaching and sharing and to always picture myself standing on that roadway, listening with the deep heart's core.

The topics I present and the information I include offer a path to peace as well as sharing tools for processing and coping with grief. I learned that my participants want to find peace in listening to their loved one's favorite song or gathering photographs of a family reunion or keeping their husband's work shirts, their child's stuffed bear, or the last jar of tomato sauce their mother put up.

The Program

The death of a loved one is a life-altering experience with permanent ramifications. After the immediate coping with the death has passed, the survivor often looks for ways to manage the ongoing grieving process. This bereavement program is designed to give those who have lost a loved one an opportunity to explore and express their grief in a spiritual environment through story, art, music, video, meditation, and activities. This program is intended to be a sequel to the traditional immediate grief support that may be offered through a hospital, hospice, or parish.

The prayers, Scripture, and guided meditations have a Christian grounding but are appropriate and welcoming to those of many faith traditions. The activities are designed to be engaging without being intimidating. One need not be a Rembrandt, Mozart, or Shakespeare to participate in the art, music, and writing activities.

The core of the program is the eight sessions that explore themes of grief and loss leading to hope, using the arts as

This bereavement program is designed to give those who have lost a loved one an opportunity to explore and express their grief in a spiritual environment through story, art, music, video, meditation, and activities.

tools. While I give you scripts for the eight-session program, "Creative Bereavement" can be tailored to your specific situation and needs. I encourage you to use the music, video, and articles that are available to you and that make sense for your group.

I have been successful at fashioning six- and four-session programs from the base of eight topics. You could easily do a five-, three-, or two-session program to suit your community.

Single sessions can be created from any of the themes or a blend of several themes. For example, for some, loss is not confined to death. Loss includes having to sell one's family home, move to a different town or state, or cope with health challenges and mobility issues. There are myriad losses to grieve, and the principles are the same. For many, committing to a multi-week program is not possible, but coming to a single session may give grievers basic information on grief and loss and some tools for dealing with both. Regardless of the format you choose or the number of sessions you offer, it is critical to always balance providing helpful information with allowing space for processing while encouraging future actions.

Prerequisites

- Schedule each session for 75 to 90 minutes plus some gathering time. Include 15 minutes for light refreshments as participants arrive.

- Welcome all grievers but encourage participants to be a year or more past the death of a loved one. It takes time to be ready to write new chapters for our lives.

- Welcome adults of any age who are grieving the loss of any loved one.

- Assure participants that they only need to share with others as much as they are comfortable sharing and to participate as much as they feel comfortable participating.

- Assure participants that no talent in the arts is needed, only a willingness to try out the activities.

Caveat: This program is not appropriate for children or youth. Their ability to process death and their psychological needs are different from adults and should be treated by professionals trained in child psychology.

Format

Each session is built around a theme. The eight themes explore various dimensions of grief and loss. Each session follows a similar structure so that participants know what to expect. Predictability creates a comfortable zone for them.

Each session is divided into four movements:

- Engage

- Learn

- Reflect

- Apply

What comprises each movement will vary depending on the topic. Each session includes:

- Review and overview

- Opening Scripture

- Meditation

- Information on grief and loss

- Video clip and response

- Reflection and sharing

- Activity and participant interaction

- Closing Scripture, reading, or song

THE EIGHT-SESSION PROGRAM

1. **Introduce Your Loved One**
2. **Tell Your Story**
3. **Holding On and Letting Go**
4. **Hear a Special Song**
5. **Visualize Your Grief**
6. **Cherish This Place**
7. **Preserve Your Memories**
8. **Plan Your Future**

Because everyone grieves differently, the program is designed as a flexible journey. It is a road that unfolds with numerous lookouts along the way that allow travelers to stop, rest, reflect, unload their pack, pick up tools or mementos, share experiences, and determine where the road will take them. While the topics have a collective effect in exploring the themes of grief, loss, identity, memory, and coping, they are self-contained and independent topics. The components of the program can be presented as a single multi-week program; a monthly presentation series; selected topics for workshops or a day of reflection; or two or three sets of a multi-week program with or without a break between sets of topics. You may wish to break for an extra week in the middle of a multi-session program to give participants an opportunity to process what they have learned and return with new insights.

Each session is freestanding, in that it does not necessarily build on the prior session. On the one hand, there is a progression from the first week to the last. On the other, if someone misses a session, they are not lost when they return. You may rearrange the sessions to suit your group. Some sessions are easily grouped in pairs (1–2, 3–4, 5–6, 7–8), which could be used as half-day retreats. Sessions 1 and 2 should be the beginning, and 7 and 8 should be the conclusion. Sessions 3 through 6 can be arranged in the order that works for your group.

As a teacher, I always want to offer knowledge. Throughout the program, you will find information about grieving. You will see the fifteen statements about grief that I explain in Chapter 4 spread throughout the sessions. The templates include a handout with this grief information. Participants want information to be shared with them, not presented as an academic lecture. Mostly, they want a safe space for processing that information. As a pastoral minister, I want to offer that space.

Let's look more deeply at the eight themes.

1. Introduce Your Loved One

Our loved ones were special people who were uniquely loved by us. This introductory week gives participants an opportunity to share their story by first introducing their loved one. We will examine how grief manifests itself in our lives. We will introduce some of the techniques used throughout the program: guided meditation; a poem on grief; contemporary songs; movie clip; sharing; and personal reflection.

Why? Participants arrive desperate to talk about their loved one. As participants introduce themselves, they often frame their introduction around their loved one. Sharing the story of their loved one sets the table for the rest of the interaction throughout the program.

2. Tell Your Story

We have lived a singular and diverse story with many characters and plot lines. The death of our loved one radically altered our story. Understanding our story can give us insights into how to imagine a new story for ourselves without our loved one. In this session, the emphasis will be on exploring a griever's version of three virtue ethics questions: Who was I with my loved one? Who am I now? Who will I become without my loved one?

Why? Participants should have the opportunity to reflect on themselves in relation to their loved one. They may be many things as individuals, but who were they with their loved one? How will they write new chapters for their lives without their loved one?

3. Holding On and Letting Go

Grievers are often urged to "let go" and "move on." However, the griever grasps for memories while struggling with the conflicting demands of the past and the future. How can we find the right balance?

Participants will bring to this session an object that reminds them of their loved one (a piece of jewelry, a greeting card, an article of clothing, a tool, or a knick-knack). We will focus on those things we wish to hold close while finding the strength to let go of those things we no longer need. The session includes a review of losses: minor and major, temporary and permanent. We will learn about patterns of grief.

Why? This session is about more than cleaning out the closet. It is about empowering participants to deal with all the well-meaning folks who want to tell them how to grieve and how to act. Further, it is about giving the participants a framework for determining for themselves what to let go of and what to hang on to.

4. Hear a Special Song

Music can evoke powerful emotions and allow us to express our deepest longings. Music can also be a vehicle for celebrating our loving relationship with the deceased. Silence, too, is a beneficial healer. We will explore the difference between instrumental and intuitive grievers as well as grief triggers.

Participants will bring in a piece of music, a list of titles, or words to a song that reminds them of their loved one.

Why? Music packs a powerful memory punch. It is not only our favorite lullaby but also that song that creeps up on us in the grocery store or the hymn that assaults us in church. Music can be an instant trigger to both sadness and comfort.

5. Visualize Your Grief

Visual arts can take us to a place or time we shared with our loved one. Visuals are a way of preserving memories and igniting hope for our future. It might be a photograph, a strip of wallpaper, or that special landscape you both loved. Treasured visuals can release thoughts or feelings we have been unable to process in other ways.

We will use samples of traditional artwork to stimulate our memories of our loved one. We will explore four of the fifteen grief statements that center on the unique experience of grief and loss.

Why? This session is designed to take a deeper look at grief to better understand our own, taking us from stress and potential despair to calmness and hope.

6. Cherish This Place

Place has a unique and powerful hold on us. Our childhood home, our school, our neighborhood, a favorite vacation spot may all be places we cherish. Place can be about special memories and a safe environment for sharing and experiencing those memories. We will study how grief manifests as well as reviewing healthy and unhealthy behaviors.

Participants will have a hands-on opportunity to creatively express their memories of special places using various media. No artistic talent is needed, just a willingness to delve in and express.

Why? The importance of place is why we have memorial gardens, benches, parks, and fountains. It is why survivors sometimes volunteer at the facility that cared for their loved one or create funds to support a school or health facility.

7. Preserve Your Memories

Our memories are sacred: sharing the goodness of the loved one is important for extended family and the next generation. Memories offer us both healing and perspective. We will explore positive ways to confront traumatic deaths as well as learn about stages of grief and resilience.

Participants will first determine which memories they wish to preserve and which ones they wish to leave behind while deciding how they will preserve and transmit those memories to others.

Our memories are sacred: sharing the goodness of the loved one is important for extended family and the next generation.

Why? Grievers have few opportunities to safely confront and discuss traumatic deaths.

This session offers a safe space for learning about residual trauma, stages of grieving, and putting grief in a context.

8. Plan Your Future

Our story needs new chapters and perhaps a new setting or new characters. It is time to answer the question "Who will I become?" We will pull all our new insights together using the labyrinth as a tool to begin rewriting our story without our loved one. This is a summarizing session that encourages participants to reflect on what they have discovered about themselves and their grief while discerning how to best use those revelations to plan their future.

Why? This session allows participants to review the whole program, to embed what they have learned, and to form a plan for moving forward into a new story.

THE SIX-SESSION PROGRAM

How might you rework the eight themes into a six-session program? One plan I have used combines Sessions 1 and 2 into one session on Story and Sessions 5 and 6 into one session on Visuals. Carefully choose the materials to use in the combined sessions. Remember to organize your sessions around the four movements: Engage, Learn, Reflect, Apply.

Session 1: Tell Your Story

Combine introducing your loved one with telling your story. The story theme prevails. Include the prayer board and the concept of the empty bench.

Session 2: Holding On and Letting Go

This is a powerful session and might be better standing alone in a six-session grouping.

Session 3: Hear a Special Song

This session on songs and music is a popular stand-alone as well. Folks love to share their favorite music.

Session 4: Visualize Your Grief

Visuals of any kind work well with the power of place theme. Using the museum cards is a good conversation starter. Include artistic reminders of a favorite vacation spot, family home, or neighborhood.

Session 5: Preserve Your Memories

This gives the group an opportunity to review information on grief and loss along with deciding how to preserve their memories.

Session 6: Plan Your Future

Getting to the hope-filled plan for the future is critical. End on an upbeat note with discussion of the possible future chapters for participants' stories.

An alternate approach leaves the first two sessions intact but combines the two visual sessions, 5 and 6, into one focused on the power of place. This iteration also combines Sessions 7 and 8 into a final session that focuses on preserving memories and planning the future.

THE FOUR-SESSION PROGRAM

Compressing to four sessions requires making choices about what is important to present to your group and what to save for another day. Focus on the key themes. Include the fifteen statements about grief. The following four-week program works well:

Session 1: What Is Your Story?

Focus on the two questions "Who was your loved one?" and "Who were you?" Include the prayer board, the bench meditation, and learning about stories with examples of how our stories have changed. Use the *Sleepless in Seattle* clip, which is packed with insights.

Session 2: How Do You Deal with Your Grief?

Focus on the themes of "Holding On and Letting Go," "Visualizing Your Grief," and the "Who are you now?" question. Include some of the fifteen statements on grief. Include participants' object reminders of loved ones and the museum card exercise if time allows. Use the *Gravity* clip and discussion of ramifications of holding on and letting go.

Session 3: How Do You Preserve Your Memories?

Focus on the themes of "Hearing a Song for Your Loved One," "Preserving Your Memories," and the question "Who will you become?" Include music and silence, types of grievers, traumatic deaths, and preserving memories. Use the *Unfinished Song* clips as well as the short clip from *Lewis*. Add the *NCIS* clips if time permits.

Session 4: How Will You Plan Your Future?

Focus on the "How do you get there?" question and hope. The "What's in Your Bag?" activity can be done here to wrap up what has been learned about grief and writing new chapters. Include any learning about grief not already covered. Use the clips from *The Best Exotic Marigold Hotel* in contrast with those from *Downton Abbey*.

SINGLE SESSIONS

As noted, single sessions can be fashioned from any of the themes or any of the activities. I have run a single session on "Coping with Grief and Loss at the Holidays" that emphasizes coping, triggers, and memories. I pull in holiday music and movie clips that highlight managing expectations versus the reality of holidays. In any single session, I always include the fifteen statements and other information about grief from the handout. Even a single session can be built around the four movements: Engage, Learn, Reflect, Apply.

3

Facilitating a Bereavement Program

"Come to me, all you that are weary and are carrying heavy burdens, and I will give you rest."
[MATTHEW 11:28]

...the fruit of the Spirit is love, joy, peace, patience, kindness, generosity, faithfulness, gentleness, and self-control.
[GALATIANS 5:22–23]

My son and my eldest daughter are Army officers. Between them, they have served seven long deployments to Iraq and Afghanistan stretched over a dozen years. They have both lost soldiers in their units, classmates, friends, and siblings of friends. Being a military mother and living those losses with them is an integral part of who I am.

One Veterans Day, I attended the veterans memorial service at the State House with my middle daughter, who worked for the governor of Massachusetts. Gold Star families—those who have lost a family member in combat—are the honored guests. They were seated in the round Hall of Flags while a brass quintet played patriotic music. We joined another staffer to watch the event from the balcony that surrounds the hall.

As the program unfolded, I had my emotions under control until the governor spoke. He began by reading an excerpt from *We Were Soldiers Once...and Young*, by Hal Moore and Joseph Galloway. My husband, an Army Ranger, knew several of the soldiers profiled in the book. The excerpt the governor read was a thank-you letter from the mother of a soldier killed in action to the family's hometown for their outpouring of support. I started sobbing uncontrollably. I could put myself in that scene. I had attended those funerals. I had talked to those parents. My daughter started crying, as did her colleague. We had to step back from the edge of the balcony lest our tears rain down on the Gold Star families. Who were they grieving? A parent, child, sibling, spouse? I thought of my late father, a Navy radioman; my cousin, an Army mechanic who died by suicide; my son's friend who was killed in Afghanistan. The stoic families, the brass music in the background, the letter, the governor himself choking up as he read. I was smothered in a blanket of sorrow and remembrance.

What Facilitators Need to Know

Why do I relate this experience? To remind facilitators that grievers are surrounded by symbols of their grief, reminders of their loved ones, and triggers. Everyone has triggers that unexpectedly set off memories. That song from your high school dances, the fragrance of your mother's perfume, the call of a seagull conjuring family vacation scenes. In the case of bereavement, that trigger sets off grieving. My hot button, that which triggers instant tears and tightening in the chest, is anything to do with the military. Any story in the news, even hearing "The Star-Spangled Banner," makes me tear up for the young lives lost.

One of the key things to understand about facilitating a bereavement program is that it is an exercise in balance. One must be able to balance all the good things that the program represents for grievers—love, joy, peace, patience, kindness, gentleness—with the facilitator's ability to exert self-control over their own triggers and lead the group to positive sharing and self-reflection. Before you can facilitate a bereavement group, you must know your hot button and understand how it affects you. Because facilitating a program like this will set off your triggers, you must be prepared to handle them. I tried once to use excerpts from the docu-drama *Taking Chance* about the journey to bring a fallen soldier home. The film spoke so well to grieving, duty, and reaching out to mourning families. However, just attempting to prepare the clip was too emotional, and I did not use it. You may be an expert facilitator, but you cannot be an effective bereavement facilitator if you cannot control your triggers.

In her book *Bearing the Unbearable: Love, Loss and the Heartbreaking Path of Grief*, Joanne Cacciatore cites the following: "By permitting an unrelieved descent into the raw emotions of grief within the secure boundaries of ritual space, hope and trust may be paradoxically restored." For grievers, finding a space where others respect their loss, their sorrow, and their vulnerability is essential. Both the leader and the other participants should be fellow travelers on the road of grief and recovery. The leader may not have experienced the same grief and loss as the participants, but the leader should not be looking in from outside the circle of grief. We can best share what we know, what we believe, and what we live.

Be a companion, be a witness, and always be compassionate. Cacciatore suggests that "it is the presence (or absence) of others who are willing to show their care for us when we are overwhelmed"—that is, the "compassionate witness"—who makes all the difference in the grieving process for the griever. It is the compassionate witness who, "listening with care and responding with compassion," can move the griever from overwhelming and paralyzing grief to focusing on actions that will be hope filled and future focused.

Are You Ready to Be a Bereavement Facilitator?

First, ask yourself, why are you choosing to facilitate a bereavement program? Bereavement work is a calling. Be attentive to the nature of that calling. Do this because you wish to be present to others in their grief, not because you drew the short straw among the staff. Do this because you can empathize with the pain of grief and loss, not because you need to work through your own grief.

Second, are you comfortable talking about grief, death, and loss? Can you listen attentively to the pain of others? Can you be sympathetic without being patronizing? Grievers are vulnerable. They are fragile. They are looking to find rest from the heavy burden of their grief. They are looking for peace and kindness and a path to joy. You should have the empathetic ear they may not find in any other setting. You can be the source of the comforting tools they may be seeking.

Finally, I cannot emphasize enough that you are probably not a psychologist, counselor, medical professional, or social worker. Even if you are one of those professionals in your work life, people are not coming to a bereavement program for those services. They are seeking peace and the companionship of other grievers. I begin each session by reminding the participants that I am not a psychologist, counselor, medical professional, or social worker. My training is in pastoral ministry, spiritual formation, grief and loss. I can offer contact information for local psychological or counseling services, but I cannot offer those services.

What Facilitating Skills Should You Employ?

Let me highlight those skills you will particularly use with a bereavement group.

Listen. Listen to your grievers with both your mind and your heart. Listen attentively to what they are really saying about their loved one, their loss, and their future.

Share. Share prudently after you have listened. This program is not about you; it is about your participants and their loved ones. You can share an experience but avoid dominating the conversation. Avoid giving advice. Offer a suggestion instead.

Question. Ask questions carefully. Questions should gently nudge grievers to a deeper understanding of their grief or current situation. Get to know your grievers' loved ones through questioning that encourages stories. Form suggestions as questions. *Would it help if you did…? Have you thought about…? Do you know that…? Can you tell us more about…?*

Maintain boundaries. It goes without saying that proper boundaries must always be maintained. It is tempting to think that because your group is grieving, the traditional professional boundaries no longer apply. They do. Keep enough distance to maintain your leadership. You can be patient, kind, generous, faithful, and gentle without crossing professional boundaries.

Be yourself. Be who you are. Be open and honest. Do not try to take on a persona that you think will be effective.

Be honest. Be comfortable admitting when you do not know something. Avoid trying to put a happy spin on everything. Honesty is more helpful than a false sense of optimism.

Be positive. Try to maintain a positive outlook without being a Pollyanna. Reminding grievers that they have the strength to get through this difficult time is helpful. The sun will shine again, but it may take a long time to see it emerge through the clouds.

Smile. Never underestimate the soothing value of a simple smile.

What Facilitating Skills May Be Unique to Bereavement Groups?

Be present. Listen, gently ask questions, allow silence, encourage sharing. You cannot fix anything for the grievers who participate in your program; do not try. You can, however, be an understanding ear.

Know the loved one. Those who grieve need to tell the story of their loved one, to share who that person was. They want the person to be known and remembered. Ask questions that help the participant flesh out the loved one. Your participants' deceased loved ones will become the unseen members of your group. Welcome them and get to know them.

Know the griever. With gentle questioning or astute listening, get to know your participants. What else is going on in their lives? What is influencing their grief? How are they handling their grief? Help them recognize subtle influences on their grief so they can better address them.

Be supportive, not judgmental. Remember, ask questions or make suggestions rather than offering advice. If you want to say, *"I think you should..."* STOP! Say instead, *"Would it help if you tried..."* Facilitating is the art of patient listening and thoughtful questioning that leads the participant to deeper self-understanding.

Be prepared with referral information. Participants may ask for recommendations for local counseling, mental health, or other services. Have information about trusted services in the area ready to hand out.

Avoid platitudes and clichés. "I know how you feel." No, you don't know exactly how this person feels or why.

"This happened to my mother/sister/neighbor/coworker." No, it didn't. Not in the exact way that this griever has experienced it.

"This is God's will." Is it? Faith-based groups should not require blind faith in what one person has deemed to be God's will. That is for the griever to discern, not others.

"There is a new angel in heaven." Really? Suggesting that the deceased is now an angel is quite a leap. The griever does not want an angel; the griever wants the loved one back. When in doubt, listen!

Use your own experience in a positive way. Some personal experience, shared in a positive way, can be helpful. For example: "When my dad died, it helped the family to share happy memories together over his favorite meal." "When my sister became ill, we asked the cousins to send her funny cards."

Don't be afraid to cry. The work is draining, both physically and emotionally. It is fine to shed a tear. But pause and take a breath before you might become overwhelmed. You are the leader.

Use what is topical and familiar. Look to newspaper columns, magazines, websites and blogs, television shows, and movies to illustrate the concepts you are conveying. There is a wealth of good resources out there if you are alert to them. I find newspaper columnists the best source of current stories that will fit nicely with your themes. Using print media, television, online resources, and movies makes the information less preachy and more accessible to grievers who are looking for support, not a lecture.

Encourage continuing bonds with the loved one. Grievers are looking to preserve connections to their loved one, be it through memories, photographs, awards, or stories. Throughout the program, encourage grievers to cultivate continuing bonds—those actions that preserve cherished memories in any form. Participants may seek advice from the group on appropriate memorials. Also be open to the spiritual presence of the loved one in participants' lives, in their "deep heart's core."

Remind grievers to balance "holding on" with "letting go." I devote a full session to the theme of "holding on" versus "letting go," but it is useful to keep this theme in mind throughout the program. Remember:

"Letting go" is not the same as "moving on."

"Moving on" feels like abandonment and forgetting.

"Letting go" is treasuring memories but not letting them cripple you.

There is a time to hold on and a time to let go. Only the griever knows when.

Hold on to what gives comfort. Let go of the stuff that no longer matters.

Focus on hope. Throughout the program, hope should be one of the underlying themes. Not the feel-good greeting card versions of hope but the virtue of hope that is action in our lives. Hope that is sustaining. Hope that can move us to a new reality. I use the virtue ethics work of moral theologian James F. Keenan, SJ, to illustrate the hope we should project to our grievers. In *Virtues for Ordinary Christians*, Keenan writes: "Whatever enables us to continue to believe in the face of death, doubt, uncertainty, or fear, is hope."

How Do You Manage Your Group?

As with any program, there will be challenges. The person who monopolizes the conversation. The person who asks so many questions you cannot keep up with the racing thought process. The person who veers the conversation off track. Pulling individuals together and keeping them on topic can feel like herding cats. (I know because I have a cat.)

One may feel comfortable managing the dynamics of a book group or political discussion group. However, one may be less inclined to firmly manage grievers, thinking that they are already sad and fragile, so you do not want to further upset them by curbing their conversation, questions, or tangential stories. In some ways, because your participants are fragile, you need to be even more in control of diversions that can undermine the comfort of the group and the flow of the program. Always balance the challenges with the rewards. You will also see that participants willingly comfort others and form bonds that extend outside of the group, giving of themselves unselfishly. Manage a bereavement group with a strong, velvet-gloved hand—firmly but with the feel of softness. If you inadvertently cater to one or two participants, you can end up alienating the others. Gently encourage mutual support and shut down diversions.

Let me share some typical challenges that can derail a program and then some positive experiences that can enhance it.

There is the chronic latecomer who wants what has transpired to be repeated. Gently say that you will repeat material at the end of the session. Worse is the latecomer who bursts into the quiet meditation and attempts to assume control of the session. Here is where using body language and a firm statement to exert leadership is important. Stand, make eye contact, and take the floor while firmly stating, "Grab a seat and we'll hear why you were delayed later."

Similarly, a slightly raised "stop" hand gesture or a firm look can quiet the person who interrupts others. Continue the program as if nothing had happened.

At the beginning of the opening session, I always outline some rules for the group. You will find them in Session 1. I learned to include the obvious reminder to latecomers to enter quietly. I also learned to articulate behavior expectations much more clearly. Participants can be nervous, since this experience is very personal, and that uncertainty can reveal itself in weird behavior. I remind folks that while they may be delayed, they must respect the group and the moment. As my mother used to say, "Do not interrupt unless you're bleeding."

The flip side, however, is those who unexpectedly share a personal experience or revelation and transform the group into the sacred sharing space it should be. One of the first groups I facilitated was a gathering of Catholic women meeting in a Catholic parish hall. I had a Jewish neighbor who, by happenstance, learned of the program and asked to attend. Her husband had died a year earlier, and she was approaching the end of the Jewish mourning period. Throughout the sessions, she willingly shared with us the Jewish rituals around dying, death, and grieving. She added a dimension that broadened our perspective and enriched the experience for everyone.

Similar was the eureka moment when one member came to the music session bursting to tell us that with her brother's help, she had accessed her late husband's iTunes playlist, which she had feared was locked away forever. She was so grateful to have his favorite songs to enjoy. You cannot orchestrate every aspect of your sessions, but you can balance controlling disruptive behavior with facilitating unexpected enriching behavior.

What Happens When a Participant Dies?

Bill was an active participant in a bereavement drop-in group I led at the local senior center. He was a retired widower who was showing early signs of dementia and a valued member of our group, eager to hear everyone's monthly updates while adding the male perspective to a predominantly female group. He had triumphantly related to us how he had beaten cancer, so his unexpected death seemed so unfair. One month he was with us and the next he was not. How does the facilitator handle this experience?

As soon as I learned of his death, I emailed the group to let them know. I followed up with the wake and funeral details and invited those who were comfortable doing so to attend. The next time we met, I opened the session by talking about him, mentioning some of his amusing observations and inviting others to share memories.

Then we continued with the session. When dealing with a death among the group, sensitively acknowledge it but do not dwell on the loss. I occasionally mention something that Bill shared with us, but I do not allow him to become the center of our meeting. As with so many aspects of facilitating, it is about balance.

What If the Group Wants to Continue after the Program Ends?

After my first eight-week program, members of the group wished to keep meeting. I was excited that they wanted to continue supporting one another. However, I was reluctant to take on another task. We worked out a compromise. I would facilitate a monthly session where the group could gather to share their ongoing experiences. There would be no program, and members of the group would provide any refreshments. One member offered a meeting space in her church, where we met for a year, eventually finding space in our local senior center. The bereavement drop-in was born. Once a month, I was present for 75 minutes at a convenient time for participants. The center advertised the group. People came as they wished. No commitment. Some stayed for years. Some came occasionally. Some came for a while and drifted away. The group has been a touchstone of support for many but not a significant commitment for me. Balance!

Can You Care for Yourself?

Caregivers and program facilitators need care just as grievers do. We are all busy; we all work hard, often long, irregular hours. Facilitating a bereavement group can be draining. Make sure you take time to care for yourself. Know when to reach out for help, even if the help is as simple as having someone else set up refreshments or do the advertising. Find a counselor or spiritual advisor to be your outlet and your sounding board. A rundown, emotionally drained facilitator is not helpful to a group of grievers. Don't forget to save time in your schedule for healthy activities and quiet time. Know your limits and find positive coping strategies when you are stressed. Most important for bereavement facilitating:

- **Be self-aware.** Be aware of your own history of loss and grief. Your losses may determine when you are ready to facilitate a bereavement program. It is perfectly fine to step back if you are not ready. You may even want to have a backup person or a partner who can step in to handle a challenging participant or take over a portion of the program that may be difficult for you.

- **Balance! Balance! Balance!** Balance holding on and letting go. Some things are obligations and must happen, like grocery shopping. Other things, like scheduling one more meeting, are not and have to be let go.

Throughout your program, remember that grievers will present you with emotional stories, disturbing situations, and deep sadness. You cannot carry these stories home with you and allow them to weigh on you. You may need some help processing others' stories so you can continue to be an effective leader. The responsibility of holding those stories should not fall entirely on you. Invite the larger community of faith to support and care for the bereaved. Ideally, your bereavement program is a part of a larger array of services that your parish provides for the grieving. If not, work with your parish community to expand the services, rituals, and support for the bereaved.

Finally, you are a skilled leader. You have the kindness, generosity, faithfulness, gentleness, and self-control to facilitate this program. The gifts you bring to grievers will far outweigh the challenge of putting the program together. Take a deep breath and begin!

4

What Should You Know about Grief?

Do not fear, for I have redeemed you;
  I have called you by name, you are mine.
When you pass through the waters, I will be with you;
  and through the rivers, they shall not overwhelm you;...
Do not fear, for I am with you...

[ISAIAH 43:1–2, 5]

My first adventure after my husband, Brian, died was a two-week trip to England. I called it my breakout tour. My eldest daughter, an Army major at the time, was posted at England's Royal Military Academy Sandhurst as the American exchange officer, living in a house abutting the Sandhurst reservation, thirty miles southwest of London. One of my widow friends and I flew over that April, used her house as our base, and traveled throughout the south of England, mostly by train.

Unexpectedly, our vacation featured a series of experiences of death, grief, and loss that illustrated the varied nature of grieving. Our first week in England, former prime minister Margaret Thatcher died. The official pomp and circumstance of her funeral was a world news event. The British rituals for the death of a public figure were historic and well defined.

Two days before we came home, the Boston Marathon was bombed near the finish line. My other two daughters were spectators at Mile 24. The trauma of the Marathon bombing was the ongoing horror of the deaths and the maiming of innocent people watching a race on a spring holiday. Ultimately, many survivors of the Marathon bombing became examples of resiliency and of turning tragedy into something life-giving for others.

My personal experience was more nebulous. One day we visited Salisbury Cathedral, with its soaring central spire. The high Gothic architecture seems to lift you up on the breath of its lightness. The wide, sunlit space of the west end is dominated by an unusual baptismal font, a four-cornered, ten-foot-wide water sculpture created out of stone and copper. The water, like an infinity pool, flows over the edges of the corners in a continuous waterfall through grates in the floor. No matter where you stand, you see the reflection of the stained-glass windows in the water. It was mesmerizing. Between the corners are concave copper bands inscribed with Isaiah 43:1–2.

I was overwhelmed with the message I absolutely believed was for me: "I will be with you." Darkness and loss answered with light and hope. Leaving the font, I walked up the north aisle to find a stained-glass window memorial to World War I soldiers, inscribed with another Isaiah citation (40:31): "They shall mount up with wings like eagles, they shall run and not be weary, they shall walk and not faint." From the first reading I chose for Brian's funeral. I felt hugged by Brian.

Grieving is very hard. Public or private, historic or personal, traumatic or soothing, grieving can overwhelm us. We can turn off the television and walk away from public tragedy, but we live with the deaths of our loved ones constantly. Triggers surprise us when we least expect them. But so do messages of comfort. We wrestle with grief and loss in the strangest places. However, we can find comfort there as well.

Grief and Facilitating

As you prepare to facilitate a program on bereavement, here is a crash course on grief, grieving, and grievers. Being aware of what grief is and how it affects grievers is critical to facilitating a bereavement program that is both empathetic and informative.

Grief is a process: a journey toward gradual acceptance of the death of someone we loved. Ideally, that process moves from darkness and devastation to light and hope. Painful as it is, that process should inspire a movement toward the future. We can use many metaphors for that process, including grieving as a journey, a story, a labyrinth, etc. Throughout the sessions, I draw on analogies from these metaphors. Melissa Kelley, in *Grief: Contemporary Theory and the Practice of Ministry*, cites the work of psychologist Robert Neimeyer when she suggests: "The affirmation and/or reconstruction of meaning after loss [is] 'the central process' in the experience of grief." Grieving, therefore, is the work of finding meaning in dying and death. The goal of your program should

be to facilitate your grievers' search for that meaning.

Questions and Story

Throughout the program, keep two themes in mind: Questions and Story. The Questions are the three overriding questions posed to the participants. Story is the metaphor used for making tangible their journey through the questions.

QUESTIONS

Death interrupts everything that is familiar. To regain some stability and direction, healthy grieving invites the griever to ponder these three questions:

- Who was I with my loved one?

- Who am I now?

- Who should I become without my loved one?

These questions flow from the virtue ethics questions posed by moral philosopher Alasdair MacIntyre in *After Virtue*: Who am I? Who ought I to become? How do I get there? Inviting grievers to understand that they had one identity with their loved one and now they have another, different identity helps them to see that grieving is a process, a movement from one place, one reality, one identity to another. This program aims to help grievers find a path to creating and embracing their new identity so they can write new chapters for their lives.

STORY

The answers to these questions—Who was I with my loved one? Who am I now? Who should I become without my loved one?—form a story of the griever and the deceased. Story is an easy metaphor to use throughout the program. Stories can make meaning out of confusion, can comfort us, can allow us to see ourselves at a safe distance. Stories can provide us with a map, a "How do I get there?" by identifying the theme, plot, setting, and characters in our story. Grievers knew who they were with their loved one. Now the story demands that new chapters be written to determine who they *are* and who they *will become*. Telling the story helps to identify what has changed and where to go with it. This program gives grievers the safe space to share their story and to explore who they wish to become.

Where Is the Griever?

Grievers live in a strange "middle" place. Trauma specialist Shelly Rambo describes this middle place as Holy Saturday. Grievers have endured the suffering of Good Friday but have not yet experienced the joy of Easter

Sunday. Holy Saturday is the undefined place in the middle. The goal of this program is to give grievers tools to start to let go of the trauma of Good Friday and move toward the new life of Easter. Understand that the trauma, suffering, and sorrow of the death will always be present and always be part of one's story. Experiencing Holy Saturday is a necessary part of the grief journey. Grievers' lives have been permanently altered by the trauma of death. However, it does not mean they are doomed to live in a middle ground that replays the loss without some hope of a new and different life. Easter resurrection is not a return to life as it was; it is a hope-filled entry into a new life.

There is no timetable for moving through this middle zone; grievers should not be pushed or intimidated to "move on" or "get over it" until they are ready. Healthy grieving depends on the griever's ability to walk through the gray middle space at their own pace. However, the middle space is not where people should dwell indefinitely, referencing everything in their lives to the death of the loved one. A bereavement program may be one tool to awaken in them their desire to reach for Easter and to find, once again, joy in their lives, to move bravely through the middle, through the rivers and the waters, the fire and the flame, to hear their name and find their place of redemption.

What Is Grief?

Here are fifteen statements about grief that I use in all iterations of the program. It may be helpful to review these grief facts before you begin to facilitate your program.

1. Grief helps us to find a new reality.

The work of grieving is to find a new reality for your life. Acknowledge the loss, grieve the loss, and strive to find what will become your new life. The place at the table will always be empty. The new reality might be to create a different menu. The rituals you shared at Christmas, on July 4th, or on birthdays may be too painful to continue, or they may be a warm reminder of happy times. Finding new activities or creating new rituals can be a life-giving choice. On the first Christmas after the death of his wife of sixty years, a man in a group I facilitated served dinner in a soup kitchen on Christmas Day with his daughter and her family. He believed that serving others helped him through that painful day. There will be many "firsts": first holidays, first birthday, first summer, and more. There will also be seconds and thirds and fourths. Finding a new and comfortable reality can help grievers manage the firsts and be able to move onto the seconds, thirds, and fourths.

2. Grief is not a pathology.

Death is a normal part of life. Grief, therefore, is not an illness to be cured or an injury to be healed. Grief is an ongoing experience of loss. One does not get over it. One learns how to live with it in a better way each day. However, grief should not be destructive to the griever or to others. In working with your group, be alert to extreme anger, talk of self-destruction, expressions of revenge, or other dangerous behavior. Have contact information for trusted mental health professionals ready to share with participants who might exhibit concerning tendencies.

3. Grief is different for everyone.

There is no wrong or right way to grieve. Every person's loss and every person's grief is unique, not experienced in quite the same way as others. Avoid beginning a comment with *"You should..."* You don't know what that person should do. Instead, pose a question: *"Have you thought about doing...?"* or *"Have you tried...?"* Open the door for the griever to consider various strategies or actions rather than giving the griever orders. Remind grievers to gravitate to those who welcome them as they are and to avoid those who want to tell them how they should change. Loving advice is helpful but "You should do" mandates are not.

4. Grief has no prescribed stages.

Elisabeth Kübler-Ross' landmark work on the stages of dying is valuable but not a rigid guideline for grieving. She offers good insights on phases that we might experience following the death of a loved one, but her stages were never meant to be strictly followed, like a recipe. Some grievers will experience all the stages, roughly in the order she outlines them, but many will experience only some stages in a random order and for varying lengths of time.

5. Grief has no timeline. Grief is an ongoing process.

Grieving is not magically over in six months or a year or five years. Grieving takes a long time. Grievers are asking themselves every day: What comes next and how do I deal with it? Those around the griever may press for the person to "get over it," but loss stays with us forever. In some cases, reconciling the mounds of paperwork that seem to accompany death can delay the onset of grieving. It is why the second year after the death of a loved one is often the hardest. The reality sets in when all the immediate minutiae of death are completed. How we incorporate the loss into our daily lives, learning to better live with it, is what matters.

6. Grief is personal and intimate.

Your response to your loss is personal to you and influenced by your own background. Everyone who has lost a loved one, a house, a job, or their health is not having the same experience. No one truly knows what the griever is experiencing. Grievers' relationships with their loved one influence their grief. One person's joy is another's sorrow. Hearing the national anthem reminds me of my children's Army service, but for someone else, "The Star-Spangled Banner" might evoke treasured memories of trips to the baseball park.

7. Grief manifests in numerous and varied ways.

Grief is not revealed only in sadness. Grief can manifest in substance abuse, workaholic behavior, irrational fears, withdrawal, depression, and dangerous risk-taking. It can also inspire charity, new hobbies, new friendships, and new activities. Grievers may have difficulty expressing their feelings in publicly acceptable ways. Inappropriate emotional displays such as extreme anger or joviality often mask fear, loss, or sadness. I remember having a meltdown in my bank after my husband died because the customer service representative was lecturing me about the law on joint savings accounts. My husband was dead and so was the account she was unceremoniously closing. After my parents died, I had a similar encounter over a safety deposit box.

8. Grief has triggers.

Grief can be triggered unexpectedly, sneaking up on grievers when they least expect it, which can result in a powerful burst of emotion. The song in the elevator, the photograph on the dresser, the child on the swing, the roses in the backyard can trigger a bout of sadness. I shed more than one tear in the supermarket when the ubiquitous piped-in music included a song of special significance to a loved one and me. It can be unsettling but can also be turned into a surprise memory of the loved one, an unexpected gift to treasure rather than fear.

9. Grief affects your body and your mind.

Grief can make you distracted, fuzzy, and forgetful. Those around you may be noting how confused you seem or how sloppy you have become. You are simply overwhelmed. Grievers should not be afraid to step back occasionally, taking extra time or space without locking themselves in their rooms. Grief can disrupt your sleeping and eating as well as other routines, like exercise. Grievers may take on additional family responsibili-

ties in the aftermath of the death. There are days when making a peanut butter sandwich or finding two socks that match can be a challenge.

10. Grief requires resilience and coping skills.

Suggesting that one immediately bounce back from loss is unreasonable. Patience in allowing yourself to grieve will foster resilience. Grievers have good days and bad days, and those emotional swings will be evident in the group. The participant who was able to laugh while relating a story about her loved one during one session may be convulsed in tears for most of the next session. Those who do well over a long period of adjustment are those who derive comfort from the positive memories of the deceased; have a strong support system; develop good coping abilities; are adaptable; and are able to make something good of their new situation. This program should be one of those support systems. Coping with the stress of the loss itself plus coping with the stress of finding the new reality—new roles, relationships, and responsibilities—can be very challenging. The coping is often done alone, rendering it even more stressful. Your group should be a source of strength and support to ease the lonely burden of coping.

11. Grief may be the result of both trauma and loss.

The death of a loved one is a terrible loss, but if that death was the result of trauma—such as an accident, violence, stillbirth, drug overdose, suicide, or homicide—the dying and death itself may have produced a traumatic reaction in the griever not unlike post-traumatic stress disorder (PTSD). The griever may not reveal intimate or traumatic details of the loved one's death. Be cautious and gentle in approaching participants until they are ready to share their story with the group. Respect that they may not wish to tell the whole story. Work with the fragments they are comfortable revealing. Be prepared with referrals to professional services.

12. Grief does not happen in a vacuum.

Be aware that death happens to people while they are trying to live the rest of their lives. The griever may already be coping with illness, disability, family crisis, financial uncertainty, relocation, a troubled child, caregiving responsibilities, or other challenges. I recall having to quickly close out my parents' apartment. I put everything in storage because I could not cope with sorting, selling, and donating their belongings. Settling a complicated estate, selling a business, or dealing with contentious relatives and business partners can be extremely stressful.

The death of the loved one puts an additional strain on an already overburdened person.

13. Grief denied or repressed will emerge eventually.

Grief will eventually make itself known, maybe years after the death of the loved one. Delayed grief can manifest in destructive or debilitating ways. Some grievers never incorporate the loss into their lives in a healthy way. This is especially true with the death of a child. Being unable to accept the loss can negatively affect all members of the family. The facilitator may encourage these grievers to seek support from mental health professionals. However, avoid making this an issue or badgering them to seek help. Planting the seed is all you can reasonably do, despite whatever need for professional intervention they might exhibit.

14. Grief can be about places, pets, and relationships.

The loss of a home, a loved one's friend, or a beloved pet are felt acutely by grievers. People who are forced to sell their homes just before or after the death of a loved one are just as traumatized by their loss of the house and familiar neighborhood as the death. Ancillary loss, such as a connection to the loved one's friends or an activity shared only with the loved one, can be equally emotional. Grievers may become involved in a school or hospital they associate with their loved one as a way of staying close to that person. The loss of a child can be particularly difficult as the parents and siblings watch the child's friends continue to grow, thrive, and achieve. Loss of a beloved pet can be traumatizing for someone already mourning a loved one.

15. Grief requires meaning making.

Loss can initially be unfathomable. Part of the healing process is being able to step back, look at what happened, and figure out how one's life will move forward in light of the loss. Grief should help us evolve from confusion and sorrow to processing and reflection to acceptance and peace. The griever should move from *Why did this happen?* to *What will I do with it?* Like the Mary Oliver poem "The Uses of Sorrow," the griever searches to find the gift in the darkness of the empty box, for only then will life take on new meaning.

When my husband died, an elderly Jesuit priest reminded me that grief is the cost of commitment. The greater my love for him, the greater the pain I would feel for his death. Deep commitment comes with a price tag: the deep pain one feels after the death and the struggle to make meaning out of it. That priest was right.

Types of Grief

Those who study grief have defined many features and styles of grief and grieving. As members of your group begin to interact, you will recognize some of these features.

INTUITIVE OR INSTRUMENTAL GRIEVERS

As you get to know the members of your group, you will note that they fall loosely into two categories of grievers: intuitive and instrumental. Kelley cites the work of Terry Martin and Kenneth Doka to explain:

Intuitive grievers are emotional, willing to talk about their loved one and their sadness, grieving through outward displays of emotion.

Instrumental grievers are stoic and not particularly talkative. They grieve through actions, work, study, and projects. They are often workaholics who throw themselves even deeper into their work or a hobby, experiencing grief as a problem to be solved.

Many people are some combination of both styles of grieving. Without stereotyping, be alert to gender differences in styles of grieving.

GRIEF PATTERNS

Grief has recognizable patterns. Researchers' understanding of these patterns has evolved. You may recognize three primary patterns:

- *Common grief* is the emotions we experience immediately following the death of a loved one that slowly dissipate over time.

- *Chronic grief* is the experience of intense emotions following a death that continue with intensity over time, with no diminishment.

- *Delayed grief* is a minimal emotional response after the death that increases in intensity as time passes, often with negative consequences for the griever and those around that person. Delayed grief can become so much a part of the griever's personality and behavior that others do not even recognize it as grief.

You may also observe that grievers experience varying patterns of depression following the death of a loved one. And, conversely, they may exhibit patterns of resilience. Researchers note that patterns of depression or resilience can be the result of an individual's other life experiences.

CONTEXTS OF GRIEF

Death and grief can take place within both a cultural and a religious context. That context may be formed by family members, a cultural or religious community, or long-cherished customs. Both culture and religion impose expectations on our grieving. Grief and death rituals are acted out in both a cultural and religious context. Think of the funeral rituals you may know, such as the stereotypical Irish wake; the practice of Jewish families sitting shiva; military burial rituals; the New Orleans funeral procession; the Mexican Day of the Dead remembrance; African community public demonstrations of grief.

In religious terms, how we grieve can be tied to our understanding of God. If we view God as a loving parent or friend, we may feel increased comfort, strength, and hope from our faith. If we know God as judgmental, we may feel increased guilt and alienation over the death of a loved one.

In today's society, families seem to be drifting away from traditional wakes and funerals held in religious settings. They no longer find personal meaning in these rituals. This is unfortunate, since the experience of a wake or visitation coupled with a funeral or memorial service can be a rich source of comfort for the grievers as well as a remembrance of the deceased. Participants in a bereavement group may be looking for what they missed without a ritual for the burial of their loved one.

What Is Your Mission?

Your bereavement group is a valuable ministry. If you become subsumed in the logistics of setting up the group, remind yourself of the reason for a bereavement group: to provide grievers with the safe place to cry, someone to listen, peace for reflection, and support for finding their new reality.

"Someone I loved once gave me a box full of darkness. It took me years to understand that this, too, was a gift." Encourage grievers to find the gift in the sorrow and run with it.

5

Preparing for Your Program

Thus says the LORD:
Stand at the crossroads, and look,
and ask for the ancient paths,
where the good way lies; and walk in it,
and find rest for your souls.

[JEREMIAH 6:16]

My mother-in-law was one of the most generous, open, and welcoming persons I have ever known. Her virtue was hospitality. Friends, family, and perfect strangers were always welcome in her home. Grandchildren lived with her. They brought home friends and roommates. She embraced and fed everyone. I have a memory of teenagers in sleeping bags strewn around the first floor of her Victorian home. With the echo of a Queens accent, barely five feet tall, nothing fazed her.

What did she always provide for family, friends, neighbors, and strangers? A safe and welcoming space. That is what grievers are searching for as well. A safe space with others who understand what they are feeling. A group who welcomes them and wants to hear their story. A group who is not afraid to share tears and laughter. My program logo is an empty bench with Jesus' words from Mark 6:31: "Come away to a deserted place all by yourselves and rest a while." That should be the goal of this program.

Where Do I Start?

For many potential facilitators, much of the detail I present here is obvious—the routine stuff you do all the time. For others, who may not have run programs in their professional or volunteer lives, I hope this chapter serves as a checklist for preparing and making your program the best it can be.

Who Should Participate?

The first year following the death of a loved one is a blur, especially if the loved one is an immediate family member. The paperwork alone takes almost a year to resolve, particularly for those who are settling an estate or selling a home or business. The details such as writing thank-you notes and choosing a headstone can be all-consuming, leaving no time for the griever to begin the personal process of grieving.

Many people find that the beginning of the second year is when the total impact of the death truly hits. Unfortunately, at that point, much of the assistance people receive immediately following the death is gone. Family and friends can become impatient with outward displays of grief or the foggy uncertainty that accompanies the experi-

ence of death and loss. The casseroles have stopped coming. The expressions of concern, the visits, and deferential conversation end. The griever is back in a world where there is little interest in continued expressions of grief.

A clip from Julian Fellowes' television series *Downton Abbey* illustrates the tension between well-meaning family and the griever. Six months after the tragic death of her husband, Lady Mary explodes at the dinner table. Her family has been pushing and pulling at her all day to get involved in running the estate in the place of her deceased husband. She finally snaps, standing, flinging her napkin to the table as if throwing down the gauntlet, declaring, "My husband is dead. Can't you understand what that means? After all he suffered in the war, he's killed in a stupid car crash. Matthew is dead fifty years before his time. Isn't that enough for me to deal with? Leave me alone!" She storms from the room.

"Leave me alone!" is what many grievers wish they could shout at folks who want them to return to "normal." However, sometimes the griever unwittingly contributes to the impression that all *is* back to normal. Grievers learn to paste a fake smile on their faces, declaring to all who inquire, "I'm fine." The griever is far from "fine." One of the goals of the program is to empower grievers to express themselves honestly (without creating a scene at the family dinner table, however). In *Ethics of the Word*, theologian James Keenan, SJ, describes his bout with cancer and wanly replying "I'm fine" to well-meaning inquirers. With advice from a friend, he finally learned to accept people's expression of concern by replying honestly, "I'm OK today" or some other qualified response that did not shut well-wishers out but did not paint a false picture of stability either.

After the first year, grievers find themselves in an amorphous middle space, caught in a no-man's-land between death and life: the death of the loved one and a full life for themselves. Death seems to stop time as well as growth

The goal of this program is to acknowledge the sorrow and trauma of the death, offer support in the present, and give the griever tools and encouragement for moving into the future.

and the ability to find the new reality. Shelly Rambo, in *Spirit and Trauma: A Theology of Remaining*, notes, "The movements of life are less certain, less prescribed...In the aftermath of a traumatic event, practices and ways of life that people knew before trauma can never be fully recovered and restored as they once were. Instead, forms of life must now emerge with death as a shaping force." The goal of this program is to acknowledge the sorrow and trauma of the death, offer support in the present, and give the griev-

er tools and encouragement for moving into the future.

Who Are Your Grievers?

As you begin your program, be sensitive to the age, gender, background, and culture of your participants. While I have tried to choose music and video clips that resonate well with a broad spectrum of participants, you may wish to change out some of the music, video, or poetry to better suit your constituency. Be alert to who your participants are grieving—a spouse, a parent, a grandparent, a sibling, a child, a good friend, or another relative. An emphasis on losing a spouse may alienate those who are mourning a parent or friend. Also, note that men and women tend to grieve in different ways and will respond differently to the activities.

Think of this program as a template. Tailor the details of your sessions to the needs of your grievers. The themes remain the same, but the individual pieces that explore the theme can be changed out for pieces that speak to the interests and backgrounds of your group.

How Do I Prepare?

Careful preparation for your bereavement program will set the tone for the sessions. There is a fine line between being a slave to the material and totally winging it. Be prepared! Grievers will throw you enough unexpected questions, concerns, and emotions to which you must respond quickly and deftly. Don't allow the material to be another unknown.

As you prepare, the advertising, group size, choice of place and time, hospitality, and ambience should all make the griever feel welcome and comfortable. Consider the following:

ADVERTISING

Get the word out about your program broadly and well in advance of the sessions. Give people time to block off dates in their busy calendars. Perhaps set up a closed online group to use for communicating. Send out a welcome message before the first session and send reminders for subsequent sessions.

Keep the information in your advertising simple and straightforward. Decide on a logo, symbol, or picture that you will always use on your advertising. People will come to associate that with your program. If they do not participate the first time you offer it, they may sign up the next time.

GROUP SIZE

This program is meant to allow participants ample time to share and converse with each other. Keep the number of participants between six and twelve. Fewer than six people does not allow for a variety of interaction and puts pressure on individuals to talk more than they may be willing to. More than twelve becomes unwieldy and does not allow enough time for everyone to participate. Any group of individuals will have those who are chatty and outgoing, those who are shy and reserved, and folks in between. Participants will need to find their comfort level within the group. Six to twelve participants make that a manageable task for you, the leader, and comfortable for them.

SPACE

Choose the meeting space carefully. Is it big enough for your group but not cavernous? Is the seating comfortable? Are tables available for refreshments, supplies, and those parts of the program that will require workspace? Is it warm/cool enough so that participants will be comfortable for ninety minutes? Is the space quiet—not next to a school playground or ventilated with loud blowers or heated with banging pipes? Is the lighting bright but dimmable for meditation and video? Are there adequate electrical outlets for your media equipment or coffee maker? Does it have wireless internet access if you plan to access websites or online media? Is the space close to bathroom facilities and easily accessible for people with limited mobility? Can you post signage to lead participants to the space? These concerns may sound trivial, but if you and the participants cannot function comfortably in the space, the sessions will become a trial rather than a comfort.

TIME

Determine what day of the week and time of day/evening will best serve potential participants. Older or retired folks may be more comfortable coming to a group that meets in the daytime. Conversely, younger ones or those with young children may prefer an evening time. Weekends are a good option to entice many different ages and backgrounds to participate, especially in a parish setting. Consider seasonal changes in daylight hours as well. A group may be very willing to meet in the early evening in spring and summer but reluctant to come out after dinner in the dark months of winter.

Can you dovetail these sessions with other activities in the venue? For example, can you hold bereavement sessions for parents while their children are in religious education classes? Can you offer child-care, perhaps by tapping youth groups or teens needing community service hours? Can you offer sessions in a seniors' center before or after lunch, aerobics, or blood pressure clinics? One seniors' center scheduled my program after the weekly "Learning to Meditate" class. It was a perfect lead-in. Grievers will be more interested in participating in a program that is held at a convenient day, time, and place.

HOSPITALITY

Hospitality is an integral part of this healing process. Knowing that others care enough to greet you with refreshments is welcoming. Build fifteen to twenty minutes into the program for refreshments, especially at the first session. This is the time for you to greet participants as they arrive and for participants to introduce themselves to each other. Depending on the time of day or evening, refreshments might be coffee, tea, water, or juice; pastries, cookies, cheese and crackers, and fruit. Try to make the setup simple but attractive with pretty napkins or a colorful tablecloth. Set things up with an eye toward ease of self-service both before and during the session. I always invite folks to refill their cups or plates during the session as needed. Sometimes, when the topic evokes strong emotions, it helps participants to be able to step away from their seat and take a breather. Offer decaffeinated drinks, especially in the evening. I often bake goodies for the first and last sessions as a sign of my personal involvement.

SETTING UP

For each session, come to the venue early and set up all the equipment and supplies. Test the equipment for volume and sight lines. If you are using equipment that belongs in the venue, make sure you know how to work it in the dark without your reading glasses! The program requires access to video clips and the ability to project them. Having the necessary equipment is essential.

When participants walk into the space, have the lighting at a warm, not glaring, level and have a table set up with blank name tags and colored markers so they can create their own name tag. Have soft instrumental music playing in the background. Have the object of the session meditation at each place. For example, for Session 1, have the Empty Bench card placed at each seat. Supplies needed for each session are listed in Part 2. Many leaders like to have participant chairs in a circle for their programs. I prefer tables in a horseshoe or rectangle arrangement. This gives folks a place to put

down a cup, review a handout, and jot down a note during the session. Do what is comfortable for you. I also have a centerpiece in the middle of the chair or table configuration which includes a candle and a Bible opened to the passage for the session. Surround the candle with objects that connect to the theme of the session. (These objects are listed in each session description.)

Have a box or two of tissues strategically placed around the room. Participants may cry, and they may not have a tissue with them. Keep a few tissues in your pocket as well. You will be moved to tears by the stories of your participants. The first instruction I give to a group is that crying is not only acceptable but a natural response to the program and to our stories. Similarly, do not be afraid to laugh when something is funny. Laughter relieves tension and resets the atmosphere in the room.

A Final Thought

Do not wear black! Wear something colorful to each session. Vibrant colors lift people's spirits. You don't have to wear neon orange. Simply adding a bright tie or scarf to your outfit, a colorful sweater, or a sparkly necklace will brighten your attitude as well.

Light the candle, start the music, and break into a smile. You are ready to begin your first "Creative Bereavement" session.

PART 2

The Program

Basic Setup and Information

THIS INFORMATION APPLIES TO ALL SESSIONS.

Four Movements

Each session is broken into four movements: Engage, Learn, Reflect, Apply. This arrangement gives structure to the sessions and leads participants from exploring a particular theme, to learning more about grief and loss, to reflecting on the theme, and finally to applying the theme and learning to their situation.

Learning about Grief

In each session, some aspect of grief and loss will be addressed in a "learn" section.

In particular, fifteen statements about grief are spread across Sessions 4 to 8. Patterns of grief and types of grievers are explained in Sessions 3 and 4. The grief and loss information reviewed in each session is gathered into a handout found in the Templates and explained in Chapter 4.

Conversation

Each session includes numerous opportunities for conversation. Be flexible about using the *Conversation* breaks. Gauge your group and tailor the conversation to the available time and interest of the group by adding and subtracting questions and conversation starter statements.

Materials

Always have paper, pens, markers, name tags, and sticky dots or tape available. Give participants name tags as they arrive for each session. Materials needed for each session are noted for that session and included in the Templates.

Remembrance Board

A foam board, preferably in a pastel color, with a lettered heading such as "Our Loved Ones" or "We Remember." Sticking hearts to the board is the first activity in Session 1; taking back the hearts will be the last activity in Session 8. The board should be prominently displayed for each session.

Taking a Break

Take breaks as needed, especially if the conversation has become emotional or intense. Or invite participants to take a break when they need one. They may wish to refresh a drink or a snack in their own time.

Equipment

Equipment can make or break your session. Make sure you have appropriate equipment for video and music and that it works in your meeting space! Always set up and test the equipment before participants arrive. Check the sound and volume. Make sure you have the right extension cords, adapters, internet connections, and WiFi password. I find it helpful to have all the music for the program on a single playlist.

Resources

For most sessions, I have included more than you may need or may be able to handle. I find it is better to have more material than not enough. There is no test at the end, so use what works with your group and skip what might not work. The only absolutes are the "learn" sections about grief. You may wish to substitute a newspaper column for a video clip, use the movie version of a meditative reading, or change out a poem or song for one you found. Tailor the sessions to your group.

Video

I have chosen video clips carefully to illustrate the theme of the session. These selections give participants an opportunity to experience aspects of grief in a safe space. They can engage with the video, walk away from it, return to it, etc. You may find other clips from films or television shows that work with your group. I have provided both

scene numbers and time references where possible, along with YouTube clip titles, if available. I have also included the length of the scene in parentheses.

Music

Each session contains specific songs that complement the theme. Throughout the sessions, while participants are reflecting or working on an activity, play soothing instrumental music in the background. Songs are readily available through multiple music-sharing sites. I have a library of CDs and playlists of instrumental music that include everything from songs by local artists and university choral groups to classical music by well-known orchestras.

Poetry

Suggested poems fit with the theme of each session. Most have a spiritual dimension or hopeful theme. Use poetry that fits the theme and resonates with your participants.

Newspaper and Magazine Articles

Newspaper columns and special-interest stories can be a rich source of material from which to draw. The incidents are local and generally of interest to the participants, even years after they were published. Be alert to your own media outlets for similar material that might bring to life or illustrate well a particular theme.

Introduce Your Loved One

GOAL

Identify our loss and resulting grief and how that grief manifests.

In this session we will:

- Introduce the program, format, and materials for each session.

- Give participants an opportunity to introduce their deceased loved one(s).

- Open an awareness in the participants that Scripture, music, films, poetry, art, and meditation can offer opportunities to grieve and to heal.

MATERIALS

Activity   Heart shapes cut from heavy paper or card stock. (See Template.)

Empty Bench cards on card stock. (See Template.)

Handout with Empty Bench meditation questions. (See Template.)

Video   Sleepless in Seattle—*Scene #4, 12:45–22:19 or YouTube "Call Scene" (9:05)*

Music   "Keep Me in Your Heart" *music and lyrics by Warren Zevon*

"My Dear Old Friend" *music and lyrics by Patty Griffin*

Welcome, Introduction, Overview

"Come to me, all you that are weary and are carrying heavy burdens, and I will give you rest....I am gentle and humble in heart, and you will find rest for your souls."
[Matthew 11:28, 29b]

Facilitator Introduction

Briefly introduce yourself and share your background. Highlight whatever training or coursework you have that leads you to bereavement work. Be clear about your skills and background. If you are not a healthcare professional, psychologist, therapist, social worker, etc., state that very clearly.

Overview of the Eight Sessions

Explain that each session will:

- Have a theme related to grief and loss.

- Follow the same format, providing continuity and predictability.

- Focus on learning about aspects of grief and loss.

- Include time for meditation, sharing, and a hands-on activity.

- Include Scripture, a song, and a video clip.

- Offer a safe place to reflect, process, share, and "find rest for your souls."

Overview of Session 1

In this introductory week, we learn who our loved ones were to us. We also explore some of the techniques we will be using each week.

Ground Rules

- Respect yourself and others.

- Share both the talking and the listening time.

- Keep within the group what is shared within the group.

- Share only what feels comfortable to share when you are ready.

- Honor the silence, which is as valuable as the talking.

- Remember that everyone has suffered a terrible loss.

- Remember that all losses are equal. No loss is harder, more tragic, or sadder than any other. There is no perfect time, place, age, or relationship for death.

- Share your experience but don't give advice. One size does NOT fit all. If you want to begin a statement with "You should..."—stop. Each person grieves differently and recovers differently. Resist saying, "I know how you feel..." You don't.

- Understand that grief and loss never completely end. Eventually, we learn how to live with it.

- Slip in quietly if you arrive late, we'll get you caught up.

- Crying is OK. So is laughing!

(Remind participants about these rules as you go along, since people will slip into saying, "I know how you feel..." and "You should do....")

ENGAGE

Participant Introductions

CONVERSATION: Invite participants to introduce themselves one at a time. Ask what brought them to the group or what they hope to learn from the group.

Create the Remembrance Board

Hand out the heart shapes and markers. Invite participants to write the first name of their loved one(s) on one or more hearts. Give the group a minute to name their hearts. Play soft instrumental background music.

Who Was Your Loved One?

CONVERSATION

Invite participants to introduce their loved ones. Include the person's name, their relationship to the person, and how long it has been since the loved one died. If they are comfortable, they can share a memory of the loved one.

The facilitator begins with a self-introduction, including any recently deceased loved ones to set the tone and model what to say.

After the sharing is finished, invite participants to stick their hearts on the prepared Remembrance Board, which will be set up for each session.

PLAY: "Keep Me in Your Heart" by Warren Zevon as hearts are mounted on the board. Note that a dying Zevon wrote this song as his farewell.

Having participants get up and go to the board gives them a stretch break. Encourage them to take the opportunity to refresh their beverage or snack.

The Empty Bench Meditation

Draw participants' attention to the photo of the empty bench on the card that has been placed at each person's seat. Invite them to picture themselves in the moment described, thinking about their loved one.

> *He said to them, "Come away to a deserted place all by yourselves and rest a while."*
> [MARK 6:31]

Imagine yourself walking around a nearby pond. The walking path is wet and muddy in spring after it rains but cool in summer. The trees along the path are bright and colorful in autumn, while the path is white and crunchy in winter snow. All year round, it is a peaceful respite from the noise of the road and nearby play area. The path feels lost in nature. It is shaded by big old trees, including chestnut trees that drop their smooth nuts in spiky pods in early autumn and flowering berry trees that burst into soft white and pink blossoms in spring. There are always ducks and geese in the pond and occasionally a long-necked swan.

In a clearing at the edge of the path, between a tall ash tree and a white birch, stands a bench. It is made of wood that is the deep amber of maple syrup. The surface of the bench glows with a soft patina that feels silky to the touch. The curved seat and arms cradle anyone who stops to rest. Two can share the bench quite comfortably. When you sit on this bench, the parted bushes offer a perfect vista of the pond. Just taking a few moments on this bench makes you feel peaceful and content.

You discover that the bench is a memorial to a local resident who died on September 11, 2001. On the back of the bench is a brass plate with his name, his dates of birth and death, and a note that he graduated from the high school in 1984.

You notice that people rest on the bench. You see an elderly walker taking a break, his dog stretched out on the grass beside him. You notice people of all ages reading books and newspapers, enjoying a warm day on the bench. Often you see a couple sitting on the bench, with one person's head resting on the other's shoulder. One afternoon you observe a young man, undoubtedly a high school student, sitting on the bench with a notebook on his lap, pen in hand. He is looking intently at the pond, studying the surroundings, taking notes. You suspect he was catching up on a biology project. You think, how wonderful that people come and use this special bench. That people who never met the deceased or don't even pause to read the brass plate nonetheless find peace or, in the case of the high school student, answers by resting on his bench. This bench is a special gift to everyone who walks along the path beside the pond.

Can you picture yourself sitting on a comfortable bench, away from the demands of your life, taking just a few minutes to rest and remember? Imagine that you are on that bench now. Take a deep breath and let it out slowly. Feel the sun on your face, a cool breeze through your hair. Smell the flowering bushes. Feel the bench cradling you.

Take another breath.

Invite participants to answer the questions found in Templates in their minds or on paper.

PLAY: "My Dear Old Friend" while participants reflect and write.

Share Your Loved One
CONVERSATION

Invite participants to share what they might have written on a brass plate and why. This is your special memory and the beginning of understanding your story with your loved one. The idea of "story" will be a theme throughout our sessions. We are telling our story today with a character, your loved one, and a single word or phrase.

LEARN

The Second Year

The *Sleepless in Seattle* clip reinforces the ideas of loss, the effects of grieving, the second year, preserving memories, and beginning to move forward. The bench makes a guest appearance as well. The second year is often considered the hardest for grievers. That is when the reality of the permanent loss sets in, as you will see in this clip.

PLAY: *Sleepless in Seattle*

Note the following points as questions or statements, or invite responses:

- The Christmas setting. *Holidays are loaded with memories and difficult to navigate.*

- Sam and his son Jonah on the phone with psychologist Dr. Marcia Fieldstone. How prescient and worried Jonah is. *Jonah knows his father needs help.*

- Dr. Marcia's question: "Are you sleeping?" Sam's response after Jonah's prompting: "No." *Grieving has physical effects.*

- Sam on the bench describing his deceased wife to Dr. Marcia. *Time and space for memories.*

- His wife died a year and a half earlier. *Sam is deep into the second year.*

- Dr. Marcia: "Tell me what was so special about Maggie." Sam responds, "She made everything beautiful." Then, slowly and thoughtfully, he lists her attributes, much like I asked each one to do in the meditation. Dr. Marcia: "What do you miss?" Sam: "It's Christmas." Then describes his memories of her at Christmas.

- Dr. Marcia asks how Sam is coping. Sam's response may resonate with you: "I'm going to get out of bed each morning and breathe in and out all day. Then, after a while, one day I won't have to remind myself to get out of bed and breathe in and out."

- Note that the scene cuts away with "Somewhere Over the Rainbow."

REFLECT

CONVERSATION: Invite reactions and thoughts:

- Can you see yourself in this clip?

- What does it tell us about grieving?

- What are the challenges/experiences of the second year?

- What would you say to Sam if you could talk to him?

APPLY

Consider this statement from Elisabeth Kübler-Ross:

> The reality is that you will grieve forever. You will not "get over" the loss of a loved one; you will learn to live with it. You will heal and you will rebuild yourself around the loss you have suffered. You will be whole again, but you will never be the same. Nor should you be the same, nor would you want to.

CONVERSATION: Is Kübler-Ross' statement good advice for Sam? For you?

Closing Reflection
This poem may speak to how you are feeling. Grieving is hard!

"Experiencing Psalm 23"
(RACHEL G. HACKENBERG)

A walk "through the valley of the shadow
    of death" has poetic beauty
that does not resonate with my soul
and I resent being here.
I resist the chasm that is this heartache,
this devastation,
this loss.
I can only assume that the Shepherd's
    staff supports me
because I haven't fallen face-first
    into any pools of still water.
If there are glorious green pastures
    in the valley
I cannot see them. Death has blinded me.
"Stay with me here, sit with me"
is the only prayer I can muster.
Let the house of the LORD be here
as long as the darkest valley
    is my dwelling.
May a stream of oil make a path to find me
until I am healed and renewed
    for the journey again.

Tell Your Story

GOAL

Use the concept of "story" and the three virtue ethics questions to explore participants' unique story with their loved one.

In this session we will:

■ Understand our story and how we might begin to write new chapters for ourselves without our loved one.

■ Explore *who I was with my loved one, who I am now, and who I will become without my loved one.*

MATERIALS

Activity   Heart shapes for those who wish to add to the Remembrance Board.

Handout with story questions. (See Template.)

Video   **The Best Exotic Marigold Hotel**
YouTube "Best Exotic Marigold Hotel Trailer" (2:26)
Evelyn on her own: 0:40–2:11 and 7:30–8:30
YouTube: "Evelyn" (:47) Airport scene with son
Overview of India, Scene 5: 27:30–29:45
Evelyn at the Call Center, Scene 10 51:40–54:10
or YouTube: "Telemarketer training" 2/3 (2:41)

Music   **"Flying Home"** from *Sully* by Christian Jacob, Clint Eastwood, Tierney Sutton, J.B. Eckl

Welcome

Welcome any new participants and invite them to introduce themselves. Invite everyone to do a quick introduction of themselves and their loved one for new folks.

Review

Last session we learned about your loved one. Today we learn about you.

Briefly review ground rules. Invite participants to add hearts to the Remembrance Board if they wish.

In this session, we will explore our stories and learn how they have been altered by the death of our loved one.

Thus says the Lord:
Stand at the crossroads, and look,
and ask for the ancient paths,
where the good way lies; and walk in it,
and find rest for your souls.

[JEREMIAH 6:16]

This is our goal: to "find rest for your souls."

Guided Meditation

RUTH 1:1–4:17
Offer the following synopsis of the story of Naomi and Ruth from the Old Testament.

Naomi, her husband, and their two sons move to the country of Moab to escape famine and find work. Sadly, Naomi's husband dies, leaving her in a strange country with only her sons. The sons soon marry, but later they die as well, leaving Naomi and her two daughters-in-law, Orpah and Ruth, alone and vulnerable. Naomi decides that the three of them should return to her homeland of Judah. Not far into the journey, however, she realizes that her young daughters-in-law need to find their own security in their own land, not in hers. Her future is not their future.

So, she tells them, "Go back each of you to your mother's house. The Lord grant that you may find security, each of you in the house of your husband."

Naomi knew that her daughters-in-law were young and should find new husbands and have children with them and raise them in their own homeland. Orpah sets off for her home, but Ruth clings to her mother-in-law. Naomi urges her to leave, saying, "See, your sister-in-law has gone back to her people. So must you go also."

Ruth replies, "Do not press me to leave you or to turn back from following you! Where you go, I will go; where you lodge, I will lodge; your people shall be my people, and your God my God. Where you die, I will die—there will I be buried."

When Naomi saw that Ruth was determined to go with her, she said no more to her. They would share a new life in Naomi's land of Judah.

The story continues with the struggle for Ruth and Naomi to survive in their homeland as widows with no men to look out for them. Showing resourcefulness, Ruth is able to work for food, catching the attention of Boaz, the landowner in whose fields she gleaned. From that day forward, Boaz looks out for Ruth's safety, telling her, "All that you have done for your mother-in-law since the death of your husband has been fully told to me, and how you left your father and mother and your native land and came to a people that you did not know before. May the Lord, under whose wings you have come for refuge, reward you for your deeds." Ruth is filled with gratitude. Boaz takes Ruth to be his wife, and she soon bears him a son.

With great joy, Naomi welcomes this marriage and the son of Ruth and Boaz, for it means that Naomi now has next of kin and will be cared for into her old age. Those around Naomi recognize the great gift that Ruth had given Naomi by her loyalty.

What does the story of Naomi and Ruth tell us about loss?

- Naomi's husband died. *A main character in her story is missing.*

- Naomi's identity has changed. *She is no longer a wife; she is a widow. She is no longer independent; she must rely on her sons.*

- Naomi's sons die. *More characters lost from her story.*

- Naomi returns to her own country. *She must change the setting of her story.*

- Naomi's lifestyle has changed. *The plot of her story is altered. She cannot support herself. She has no male kin for protection and status.*

- Naomi is no longer thriving in a foreign land. *Her story theme is gone. She is now struggling in a foreign land. She can no longer share the joy of the sons with their new wives.*

LEARN

What Do We Learn from the Story of Naomi and Ruth?

- This story is not about death but about Naomi's and Ruth's agreement to write a new story together.

- Out of their sorrow, Naomi and Ruth create a new life for themselves.

- When they set off on their journey from Moab, they did not know how things would turn out for them, but they left anyway.

- Naomi gained a new son-in-law and a grandson.

- Ruth gained a husband and a child as well as a new homeland.

- They found happiness in their new story and lived a long life together.

What makes a story?

- Theme
- Plot
- Setting—time and place
- Characters—main characters and minor characters

A good story:

- Makes sense to us.

- Points to truths we recognize in the world and in ourselves.

- Teaches us something about the world and ourselves.

Let's Explore Your Story

Pass out the story questions from the Templates.

CONVERSATION: Ask participants about the variety of names they filled in. Remind them that their responses to *Who are you?* is their story. They are the main character. Now another main character, their loved one, someone on that list, is gone from their story.

Review:

- You have a unique story that is your life with your loved one.

- Your story helped you to make sense of the world. It is unlike anyone else's story.

- Your story had its crises and challenges along with its joys.

- Your story was not finished.

- How do you make sense of that story without that character?

The answer to this question is the work of grieving!

REFLECT

Let's reflect on our disrupted stories using Mary Oliver's poem and scenes from *The Best Exotic Marigold Hotel.*

"The Uses of Sorrow" – Mary Oliver

> (In my sleep I dreamed
> this poem.)
>
> Someone I loved once
> gave me
> a box full of darkness.
>
> It took me years
> to understand
> that this, too, was a gift.

SHOW: *The Best Exotic Marigold Hotel*

BACKGROUND: This movie is about starting over, but it's also about embracing new places, people, lifestyles, and traditions. A group of retired English citizens move to India to find a life they can afford—with various degrees of success.

As you watch the clips, watch for the themes of taking a risk, exploring a new life, and making it work in difficult and unfamiliar circumstances. In short, it is about writing a new chapter by looking into the "box full of darkness" and finding the "gift."

CONVERSATION: Let's review the good advice offered in the movie:

- "I've never done anything like this in the whole of my life."

- "You've never done anything at all without Dad."

- "Everything will be all right in the end. If it's not all right, it's not the end."

- "Initially you're overwhelmed. But, gradually you realize it's like a wave. Resist and you'll be knocked over. Dive in and you'll swim out the other side."

- "This is a whole new and different world. And the challenge is not to just cope but to thrive."

Can you see yourself in any of the scenes? Do you believe: "Everything will be all right in the end. If it's not all right, it's not the end."

APPLY

Writing My New Story
Can you define yourself/your story today? *Who are you?* Invite participants to answer the second set of questions in the Template.

PLAY: "Tell Me Your Story" from *Sully* as participants ponder their stories.

CONVERSATION: Invite participants to share their response to the questions.

Homework for Next Week
Bring an item (article of clothing, photo, keepsake, tool, etc.) that reminds you of your loved one or gives you comfort.

Closing Reflection
Where is your story going now? Your new story begins with the death of your loved one. Your life's calendar has been reset. Every anniversary of the death is the beginning of another year without that person.

"The Road of Life"
(JOYCE RUPP)

Another year is coming to an end.
I can feel her tug at my calendar;
I can sense her insistent movement.
I can hear her call to cross over.

Outside my window the trees are empty
and the air has the ripeness of snowfall.
I cast an inward glance to the past
and feel a deep desire to catch its glow.

Something in me wants to hold on,
to gather all the good things close to me.
A part of me that yearns for security
keeps encouraging me to grasp it all.

Then a tiny thimble-full of light
moves its way through my insecurity;
it weaves a thread of courage,
sending sparks into the dark.

Up and up it rises through my spirit
until it meets my controlling grip.
The firefly flickers of God's grace
are enough to embrace the unknown.
a surge of powerful surrender
takes over all my looking back,
and ever so gently and hopefully
I risk the road of another new year.

Holding On and Letting Go

GOAL

Discern when and how to "hold on" and to "let go."

In this session we will:

- Explore various categories of loss to better understand the grieving that accompanies them.

- Discover tools for discerning when and how to let go versus when and how to hold on, reflected in the conflicting demands of the past and the future.

- Share the object we brought to the session and why we chose to hold on to that object.

- Learn about patterns of grief.

MATERIALS

Activity   Word Cloud Posters or projected PowerPoint presentation of minor loss, temporary major loss, permanent major loss. (See Templates.)

Leaves and flower petals cut out of colored paper. (See Templates.)

Personal item brought by each participant

Video   **Gravity: Scene #4:** 29:11–37:32 or YouTube "Debris" (2:56) and "You have to let go" 3/11 (2:26)

Music   **"On My Own"** from *Les Misérables*, music by Claude Michel-Schönberg, lyrics by Herbert Kretzmer

Welcome and Review

In the first two sessions, we met your loved one and learned about your loss. We met you and learned about your story and the new chapters ahead of you.

In this session, we explore the conflicting forces of "holding on" and "letting go" in grief and loss.

Save me, O God,
   for the waters have come up to my neck.
I sink in deep mire,
   where there is no foothold;
I have come into deep waters,
   and the flood sweeps over me.
I am weary with my crying;
   my throat is parched.
My eyes grow dim
   with waiting for my God.
[PSALM 69:1–3]

The Lord is near to the broken-hearted,
saves the crushed in spirit.
[PSALM 34:18]

What Is Loss?

Use Word Clouds on Categories of Loss (see Templates). Take a few minutes to examine the basic categories of loss, which will be familiar to all.

CONVERSATION: Invite the participants to respond as you go along. Where do they see themselves? (Do this quickly. It will be self-evident.)

Minor/Everyday Loss: This does not change anything significant.

What? Show of hands: how many of you have lost something in the past week or two? Keys? Eyeglasses? Wallet? Cellphone? Tickets? TV remote? This is so annoying, isn't it?

Reaction? How does losing things make you feel? Frustrated, angry, annoyed, silly, forgetful.

Solution? How do you get past the loss? Keep important things in the same safe place. Make a plan to avoid losing things.

Major/Serious Loss: This Changes Your Life in Some Way.

Temporary—What? How many of you have experienced a temporary loss of a serious nature? Loss of mobility after surgery or illness. Relocation while home is being repaired. Children going away to college. Financial setback. Military deployment.

Reaction? How does this make you feel? Sad, lonely, frustrated, a bit depressed.

Solution? How do you get past the loss? Know the situation will get better when the person, mobility, or access to the house returns. Know the loss is temporary and resolve to make the best of it. Find new interests that will take the place of the temporary loss.

Permanent—What? How many of you have experienced a permanent loss of a serious nature? Death of a loved one? Permanent disability or chronic illness? Divorce? Lost job or career? Selling a house and moving elsewhere? Family permanently relocating far away? Financial devastation? Loss of a beloved pet?

Reaction? How does this make you feel? Very sad, depressed, lonely, at loose ends, missing part of yourself.

Solution? How do you deal with this permanent loss? That is the subject of our program today.

Loss and Grief: How Are We Impacted?

Loss affects all of us. How do we find a place for grief and loss in our lives?

We have all experienced some permanent loss at some point in our lives, such as death, illness, friends or family who move away, divorce, financial crisis, loss of a pet.

Loss requires new routines, new limits on our freedom, new responsibilities.

Profound permanent loss, such as a death, creates profound permanent impacts on our lives that last indefinitely. We may not know how to manage those impacts or how to move forward with our lives.

LEARN

What Is Grief?

"The affirmation and/or reconstruction of meaning after loss as 'the central process' is the experience of grief." (Kelley, *Grief*)

Grief is the work of remembering who we were with our loved one, knowing who we are now, and planning who we will become without our loved one.

Why Is Grieving Necessary?

- Grieving allows us to process the loss and all its ramifications.

- Grieving guides us to find a meaningful place for the loss in our lives.

- Grieving helps us to hold on to the happy memories of the loved one.

- Grieving encourages us to let go of trauma and negative memories.

- Grieving moves us to break the bonds that hold us in one place.

- Grieving inspires us to create a path to a new reality.

Patterns of Grief

Melissa Kelley's book describes three recognized patterns of grief. We should be aware of these patterns, since the unhealthy patterns may require professional assistance or intervention.

- *Common grief* is the emotions we experience immediately following the death of a loved one that slowly dissipate over time. This is a healthy response.

- *Chronic grief* is the experience of intense emotions following a death that continue with intensity over time with no diminishment. This is not a healthy response.

- *Delayed grief* is a minimal emotional response after the death that increases in intensity as time passes, often with negative consequences for the griever and those around that person. Delayed grief can become so much a part of the griever's personality and behavior that others do not even recognize it as grief. This is an unhealthy response.

Additionally, researchers note varying patterns of both depression and resilience in grievers. Long-term depression is not healthy. Those who respond to loss with resilience do well over time.

REFLECT

Holding On

Holding on and letting go is the balancing act of grief and loss. If grieving is finding the new reality for our lives, the new reality is somewhere between holding on and letting go.

CONVERSATION: Invite participants to share their item that reminds them of their loved one. Ask:

- Why do you hold on to it?

- How does it bring you comfort?

- How might it help you move into the new chapters of your life?

Holding On versus Letting Go

Let us visually explore the conflicts between holding on and letting go. What saves us? What hurts us? How do we go on?

PLAY: *Gravity*

The clips from the film *Gravity* are self-explanatory. Two astronauts—one experienced, one a novice—are thrown into chaos in their outer-space mission. They must make life-altering choices about holding on and letting go.

What did we see in these clips?

- MATT: "You're going to make it." *Future-looking*

- RYAN: "I had you." *Past-looking*

- Matt talks her into the station.
  MATT: "That's where you want to go."
  "Ever flown a Soyuz?"
  RYAN: "Only on a simulator. I crashed it." *The future is scary.*

- MATT: "You're going to have to learn to let go."
  "Say, 'I'm going to make it.'" *Positive thinking.*
  RYAN: "Radio is silent. Visuals are nonexistent." *Death is permanent.*

CONVERSATION: Reflect on the film clip. Our stories are disrupted and we have lost our bearings; we are floating in space. We want to hold on for dear life, but sometimes it is life-giving to let go.
Holding on is safe.
Letting go is scary.

Letting Go

Can we discern when it is time to let go?
Will holding on or letting go give us peace?
Letting go does not mean abandoning or forgetting our loved one.
Only we can know for sure when and how to hold on and to let go.
Nothing is more profound and more permanent than death.
Death is a leave-taking with no hope of return, reunion, reconnection, or reconciliation.
Letting go is finding the courage to write new chapters for our stories, always with the loving memory of our loved one to inspire us.

CONVERSATION: We have shared with each other what we hold on to. Can we share something we are ready to let go of? (Participants may have a hard time with this question. Give them time. Don't force a response.)

APPLY

Flower Petals and Leaves:
HOLDING ON AND LETTING GO

Pass out the flower petals and leaves (see Templates) along with markers. Invite participants to reflect on what they wish to hold on to and what they wish to let go of, then write these on the petals and leaves.

Think of the flower petals as the fresh flowers of spring that we pick and lovingly press in a book as a happy memory to hold on to.

Think of the leaves as the dry leaves of autumn that fly away with the wind and that we willingly let go.

PLAY: "On My Own" from *Les Misérables* while participants write on petals and leaves.

Closing Reflection

"The Gap"
(DIETRICH BONHOEFFER)

Nothing can make up for the absence of someone whom we love; and it would be wrong to try to find a substitute; we must simply hold out and see it through. That sounds very hard at first, but at the same time it is a great consolation, for the gap, as long as it remains unfilled, preserves the bonds between us. It is nonsense to say that God fills the gap; God does not fill it, but on the contrary, God keeps the gap empty and so helps us to keep alive our former communion with each other even at the cost of pain.

Homework

For the next session, on music, invite participants to bring a song or a piece of music to share that reminds them of their loved one. Participants may bring in music on their phone or a USB key, a list of titles, or the words to a song with a connection to their loved one. Anyone who plays an instrument is welcome to bring it as well.

SESSION 4

Hear a Special Song

GOAL

Learn about the power of music to express our grief, stimulate our memories, and celebrate our relationship with our loved one.

In this session we will:

- Explore the healing qualities of both music and silence.

- Share the songs that comfort us.

- Learn about healthy habits, intuitive and instrumental grievers, and grief triggers.

MATERIALS

Activity	**Physical or electronic access to music, written lyrics, list of songs, etc. from participants**
Video	**Unfinished Song – Scene #7** (35:45–41:38) and **#15** (1:21:45–1:27:01) Video scenes are more complete than YouTube clips:
	"Song for Marion: True Colors" (1:24) and Final Scene "A touching performance of the song"
	'Good Night, My Angel' taken from the movie Song for Marion" (3:55) 2012 film released in Britain as *Song for Marion*
Music	**"Be Still"** by the Fray, written by Isaac Slade
	"Get Me Through December" by Fred Lavery and Gordie Sampson (based on a melody by Niel Gow, "Niel Gow's Lament for the Death of His Second Wife")

Welcome and Review Prior Sessions

In prior sessions, we met your loved one and learned about your loss. We met you and learned about your story and the new chapters ahead of you. We explored the conflicting forces of holding on and letting go in grief and loss. In this session we will explore the healing power of both music and silence.

Opening Meditation:
SILENCE AND SONG

"Be still and know that I am God."
[PSALM 46:10]

PLAY: "Be Still" by the Fray

READ: abridged 1 Kings 19:4–13

[E lijah] went a day's journey into the wilderness and came and sat down under a solitary broom tree. He asked that he might die. Then he lay down and fell asleep. Suddenly an angel touched him and said to him, "Get up and eat." He looked, and found a cake baked on hot stones, and a jar of water. He ate and drank and lay down again. The angel of the LORD came a second time, touched him, and again he got up, and ate and drank. Then he went on the strength of that food forty days and forty nights to Horeb the mount of God. At that place he came to a cave and spent the night there.

Then the word of the LORD came to him, saying, "What are you doing here, Elijah?" He answered, "I have been very zealous for the LORD, the God of hosts; for the Israelites have forsaken your covenant, thrown down your altars, and killed your prophets with the sword. I alone am left, and they are seeking my life, to take it away."

He said, "Go out and stand on the mountain before the LORD, for the LORD is about to pass by." Now there was a great wind, so strong that it was splitting mountains and breaking rocks in pieces before the LORD, but the LORD was not in the wind; and after the wind an earthquake, but the LORD was not in the earthquake; and after the earthquake a fire, but the LORD was not in the fire; and after the fire a sound of sheer silence. When Elijah heard it, he wrapped his face in his mantle and went out and stood at the entrance of the cave. Then there came a voice to him that said, "What are you doing here, Elijah?"

CONVERSATION: "What are you doing here, Elijah?"

- Have you ever felt like Elijah?

- Did you think God could be talking to you?

- Do you wake up in the morning and think, "What am I doing here?"

- Is there a place for silence in our lives?

- Can we find the time and place to "Be Still"?

Music in Our Lives

Take a moment and think of the ways that music has been a part of your life with your loved one.

- Music reaches us on an unconscious level.

- Music impacts us even if we don't play an instrument or read music.

- Music allows us to safely express our feelings: sorrow, emptiness, and loss but also joy and happiness.

Psalm 98:1, 4–6

O sing to the LORD a new song,
   for he has done marvelous things.
Make a joyful noise to the LORD, all the earth.
   break forth into joyous song |
   and sing praises.
Sing praises to the LORD with the lyre,
   with the lyre and the sound of melody.
With trumpets and the sounds of the horn
   make a joyful noise before the King, |
   the LORD.

What Is Your Song?

CONVERSATION: Invite participants to share their song/music. Participants who are comfortable doing so may present, play, sing, recite, or talk about their music with their loved one. (This sharing will take a while, depending on the size of your group.)

Participants may respond to any of the following prompts:

- Why did you choose this piece?

- How does it make you feel?

- What memories does this piece evoke?

- When your loved one died, did the music stop?

- Has silence descended? Is it a comfortable, reflective silence or an empty silence?

LEARN

Music and Grieving

Music may be the perfect vehicle for understanding the two basic types of grievers as described by Melissa Kelley:

- *Intuitive grievers* express themselves outwardly, often through emotion and conversation. They willingly express their grieving though sharing stories, crying, or sad music or movies. Intuitive grievers reach out to others.

- *Instrumental grievers* express themselves inwardly, through actions. They bury themselves in work, projects, hobbies, or study. Instrumental grievers prefer to be alone.

- *Many people are a combination of both grieving styles.*

How can music bridge the gap between intuitive and instrumental grievers?

- Music can be a trigger for intuitive grievers, an expression of emotion, a uniting element with instrumental grievers who perform music.

- Music can be an outlet for instrumental grievers, giving them a vehicle for expressing emotion they share with intuitive grievers.

- Music can be both an expression and a refuge.

Grief Has Triggers

Grief can overtake you when you least expect it. Music is a powerful trigger. Music can instantly evoke emotion and memory.

Think of a song on the radio, in an elevator, in the grocery store. Suddenly, that special song is blaring in the cereal aisle. How do you feel? How do you respond?

Other triggers can include a favorite food; an aroma such as perfume, baking, or flowers; events such as birthdays, anniversaries, and holidays.

REFLECT

PLAY: "Unfinished Song"

BACKGROUND: Marion is dying of cancer but wishes to continue practicing and performing with her senior citizens' choral group. Arthur resents the time she spends with the group. He is also struggling with accepting her illness. Meanwhile, Arthur is somewhat estranged from his only son, who has his only grandchild. The choral group has been invited to submit a tape for a chorus contest, which is Scene 7—Marion's solo, "True Colors." Arthur has a very difficult time after Marion's death but eventually joins the choral group, seeking comfort. The group competes and Arthur has a solo, "Good Night, My Angel." Note the response of his son and granddaughter.

CONVERSATION: For Marion, music sustained and nourished her. For Arthur, it was sad and unnecessary. Eventually, Arthur understood the healing and reconciling power of music for both his memory of Marion and his relationship with his son and granddaughter.

Can you see yourself in Marion? Arthur? Their son? Their granddaughter?

APPLY

CONVERSATION: Invite participants to respond to the statement at the end of the movie, Scene #15: "What makes a song beautiful is not always the quality of the voice but the distance that voice has had to travel."

How does Arthur evolve from isolation and silence to making music? How else does he evolve?

Optional: Try Something New

When we hear music, we often want to dance or at least move to the rhythm of the music.

Facilitators with an interest or skills in dance, movement, or simple stretching exercises may wish to do movement with their group at this point. Movement can both release pent-up energy and emotion as well as soothe. See movement exercises in *Praying with the Body*.

Closing Meditation

We have powerful connections to music at holiday time. What was your loved one's favorite Christmas song or carol?

The song "Get Me Through December" is based on an Irish folk tune, "Niel Gow's Lament for the Death of His Second Wife." See if it speaks to you and your grief.

PLAY: "Get Me Through December"

READ: Julian of Norwich (1342–1416)

> No one listens, they tell me,
> and so I listen...
> and I tell them what they
> have just told me,
> and I sit in silence listening
> to them,
> letting them grieve.

Visualize Your Grief

GOAL

Use visuals to deepen our understanding of how grief affects our lives.

In this session we will:

- Learn how visual arts can evoke a special memory of our loved one.

- Use art to ignite hope for our future.

- Learn about the unique and healthy features of grief.

MATERIALS

Activity   **Postcards or printouts depicting art from a museum gift shop or other source.** Have an array of landscapes, still lifes, people, and places. Have at least twice as many cards as participants.

Question sheet for the museum card images. (See Template.)

Video   *Downton Abbey*, **Season 4, Episode 2,** YouTube: "A House Grieving: Mr. Carson comforts Mary" (4:13). This is a good compilation of essential scenes.

Music   **"Wishing You Were Somehow Here Again"** from *Phantom of the Opera* (music by Andrew Lloyd Weber, lyrics by Charles Hart and Richard Stilgoe)

Welcome and Review

In prior sessions, we have learned about you and your loved one, explored various aspects of grief in conjunction with holding on and letting go, and experienced the healing power of music and silence.

In this session we will explore the power of the visual arts.

"Wisdom first speaks in images."
[WILLIAM BUTLER YEATS]

Opening Scripture and Meditation

Since we are justified by faith,
we have peace with God...
and we boast in our hope of sharing the
glory of God.
And not only that, but we also boast
in our sufferings,
knowing that suffering produces endurance,
and endurance produces character,
and character produces hope,
and hope does not disappoint us,
because God's love has been poured
into our hearts.

[ROMANS 5:1–5]

O. Henry: "The Last Leaf" (ABRIDGED)

Do you recall reading stories by O. Henry in school? In 1907, O. Henry wrote a story set in an artists' colony in Greenwich Village, New York. It went something like this:

On the top floor of a third-floor walk-up, Sue and "Johnsy," short for Joanna, shared a studio. That winter, pneumonia was rampant in the city. Johnsy, from California, was small and frail, and the disease captured her quickly. "She lay, scarcely moving on her painted iron bedstead, looking through the small Dutch window-panes at the blank side of the brick building next door." One morning, the doctor told Sue that Johnsy's only chance to survive was to have something to live for. Sue declared, "She wanted to paint the Bay of Naples some day."

It was something to keep Johnsy going, so the doctor advised Sue to engage her in anything to keep her spirits focused on getting better. As the day wore on, Sue noticed that Johnsy was looking out the window by her bed and counting the leaves clinging to an old ivy vine climbing the brick wall of the adjacent building. She was counting backwards as the leaves blew away. She was down to four, and Johnsy expressed that when the last leaf fell, she, too, would succumb.

Sue was distraught and determined to give her friend the will to live, despite her fever-induced obsession with the ivy leaves. So, she pulled the shade over the window and exhorted Johnsy to rest while she tried to get Behrman, the painter on the ground floor, to help. Behrman had spent his life waiting for that perfect masterpiece to emerge from his canvas, but it never did. Behrman was often drunk and always ornery, but he sometimes posed for Sue's illustrations, as he did that evening.

When the session was over, Sue fell asleep by Johnsy's bedside, where her friend had already drifted into a deep slumber. The next morning, Johnsy demanded that Sue pull up the shade to see if any of the ivy leaves remained on their vine.

Behold, despite the fierce wind of the previous night, one ivy leaf clung to the vine on the brick wall. "It is the last one," said Johnsy. "I thought it would surely fall during the night. I heard the wind. It will fall today, and I shall die at the same time."

Somehow, the leaf hung on, and by twilight, Johnsy was convinced that she must cling to life as well. She asked Sue for broth, some milk, and a little port. While Sue cooked, Johnsy perked up and reminded her, "Someday I hope to paint the Bay of Naples."

By the next day, the doctor declared that Johnsy would survive.

Later, Sue went and found in the alley beside the building a ladder leaning against the opposite wall and paints and brushes on the ground beside it. Their neighbor, Behrman, had gone out in the dark and wind of that awful night and had painted an ivy leaf on the wall as if attached to the ivy vine. Sadly, as a result of Behrman's exposure he caught pneumonia and died. But he had painted his "masterpiece," which saved Johnsy. Why? That one little piece of art, a single painted leaf, gave her hope. And giving someone hope was the ultimate sacrifice of a friend.

CONVERSATION: What strikes you about the story? About having a future goal?

Museum Cards: What do you see?

Spread the museum art cards on a table. Invite each person to choose one card. Invite participants to respond to the Question Sheet found in the Templates.

PLAY: Play soft music while participants consider the questions in relation to their card. Begin with "Wishing You Were Somehow Here Again" from *The Phantom of the Opera*.

CONVERSATION: Invite participants to share responses to the questions about their chosen picture.

LEARN

In light of our art reflection, let us explore some statements about grief. Do they resonate with you and your experience? (See "Coping with Grief and Loss" handout.)

3. *Grief is different for everyone.*
6. *Grief is personal and intimate.*
2. *Grief is not a pathology. Grief is not an illness to "get over."*
15. *Grief requires meaning making.*

REFLECT

Grief and Hope

Like Johnsy, what allows us to go on in the face of loss? The virtue of hope. Virtues—faith, hope, love, fortitude, kindness, joy, peace, understanding, patience, and compassion—are actions. These virtues, especially hope, can be guides to managing our grief.

As James Keenan, SJ, writes in *Virtues for Ordinary Christians*,

> Hope is the Spirit entering into our tired, exhausted, fearful selves, offering us a way to continue the dialogue, to continue standing face to face with the living God. Whatever enables us to continue to believe in the face of death, doubt, uncertainty or fear, is hope. The ability to hold on, the anchor that steadies us as we are buffeted, is the presence of God in us.
>
> It is only when we are exhausted, speechless, impotent, that is, in our vulnerability, when life is darkest, that God enters us to sustain us.
>
> [Hope] is the breath of the Spirit that comes as we groan, assuring us that at our weakest moment, without any resources, God will never abandon us.

CONVERSATION: Invite participants to share:

■ Where do you find hope?

■ How does hope shape your new life without your loved one?

■ Are there other virtues that help you cope with your grief?

APPLY

PLAY: *Downton Abbey*: "A House Grieving"

BACKGROUND: Lady Mary's husband, Matthew, who was manager of the estate, was killed in a car crash the night their first child was born. Six months later, Lady Mary is numb from grief, yet her family pesters her about her future. This clip is an amalgam of scenes from this episode that tell a grief story. The table scene and subsequent advice from her grandmother and her confidant, Mr. Carson, expands on Mary's understanding of grief and finding her future. Note Isobel, Matthew's mother, lamenting that she is no longer a mother.

CONVERSATION: Can you see yourself in Lady Mary?

■ What made her snap?

■ What keeps her going?

■ How can she overcome her seeming despair? Will she choose life or death?

■ What is her grandmother's role/advice in these scenes? Mr. Carson's role/advice?

■ Is Lady Mary exhibiting any of the four statements about grief we just reviewed?

■ Can you apply any of the statements to your life?

Closing Meditation

From "For Grief"
(JOHN O'DONOHUE)

> When you lose someone you love,
> Your life becomes strange...
>
> Your heart has grown heavy with loss;...
> No one knows what has been taken
>   from you"
> When the silence of absence deepens.
>
> Suddenly with no warning,
> You are ambushed by grief.

From *A World of Curiosities*
(LOUISE PENNY)

> A loss like this was a progression of
> miseries, like stepping-stones. Until
> they reached the other side. The new
> continent. Where the terrible reality
> lived, and the sun never fully came
> out again. But where, with time and
> help, they might find acceptance
> and, with that, peace.

SESSION 6
Cherish This Place

GOAL

Explore more aspects of grief and loss while understanding the powerful hold place has on us.

In this session we will:

- Explore the power of place in our lives and in our grief.

- Review healthy responses to grief.

- Creatively express our memories, grief, and/or hope for the future using hands-on art.

MATERIALS

Activity	Crayons, markers, pastels, origami paper, play dough, colored paper, drawing paper, adult coloring book, paper strips
	Handout with Place questions. (See Template.)
Video	*The Lake House* – YouTube "Official Trailer" (2:26) "You Weren't There" Scene 7/10 (2:56) or "Best Scenes in Minutes" (7:10) is a music video featuring the song "Somewhere Only We Know" and is a good montage of "place."
Music	**"If I Could Be Where You Are"** music by Enya, lyrics by Roma Ryan

Welcome and Review

In the last session, we explored the power of the visual arts to spark memories. We learned that our grief is unique, personal, and intimate, like the pictures we examined.

In this session, we will explore the power of place to help us deal with our grief and our memories.

Opening Meditation

In the morning, while it was still very dark, he got up and went out to a deserted place, and there he prayed.
[MARK 1:35]

Place has a powerful hold on us. We sometimes desire to be in a special place. We may also desire to get away from a particular place. Place can be a mountain, a home, a room, a garden, a cottage by the sea, the facility that cared for your loved one. Boston College theology professor Benjamin Valentin suggests that place can influence our thoughts and beliefs, that we invest physical space with meaning and emotional commitment. "Places are actors, not mere settings in our lives. They are a factor that shape our story."

Has anyone read Daphne du Maurier's classic thriller, *Rebecca*? The book is about the characters and the mystery, but it is also about the place, the mansion on the coast of Cornwall, England, named Manderley. The mansion is a character in the story, not just the setting, as these passages show:

Last night I dreamt I went to Manderley again.... There was Manderley, our Manderley, secretive and silent as it had always been, the grey stone shining in the moonlight of my dream, the mullioned windows reflecting the green lawns and the terrace....

The terrace sloped to the lawns, and the lawns stretched to the sea....

As I stood there, hushed and still, I could swear that the house was not an empty shell but lived and breathed as it had lived before.

Light came from the windows, the curtains blew softly in the night air, and there, in the library, the door would stand half open as we had left it, with my handkerchief on the table beside the bowl of autumn roses.

The room would bear witness to our presence. The little heap of library books marked ready to return, and the discarded copy of *The Times*. Ash-trays, with the stub of a cigarette; cushions, with the imprint of our heads upon them, lolling in the chairs; the charred embers of our log fire still smoldering against the morning. And Jasper, dear Jasper, with his soulful eyes and great, sagging jowl, would be stretched upon the floor, his tail a-thump when he heard his master's footsteps....

When I thought of Manderley in my waking hours I would not be bitter....I should remember the rose-garden in summer, and the birds that sang at dawn. Tea under the chestnut tree, and the murmur of the sea coming up to us from the sea below.

- Places have the power to be cherished reminders of our loved ones.

- Places hold the stories we shared together.

- Places hold our memories and freeze them in time.

- Places can be where we feel our loved one's presence.

- Places can be a safe escape for grieving.

PLAY: *The Lake House* clips

BACKGROUND: The premise of the movie is a bit odd. Time as we know it is suspended. Kate and Alex, who never met, share a house on the lake near Chicago, two years apart. They communicate with each other across time by leaving messages in the mailbox. Like Manderley in *Rebecca*, the Lake House is a central character in the film.

Your Special Place

Invite participants to reflect and/or fill in the questions about special places in the Templates.

Conversation: Invite participants to share some of their responses.

LEARN

See "Coping with Grief and Loss" handout.

14. *Grief can be about places, pets, and relationships.*
12. *Grief does not happen in a vacuum.*
7. *Grief manifests in numerous and varied ways.*
9. *Grief affects your body and your mind.*

Staying Healthy While Grieving

Grieving can have a profound effect on our body. How do we maintain healthy habits? (See "Coping with Grief and Loss" handout.)

CONVERSATION: Invite participants to respond to the four statements on grief or to offer ideas and suggestions for healthy coping.

REFLECT AND APPLY

Creative Art Project

Have all your art materials laid out on a table. Invite participants to choose their medium. Have as much varied media as possible: various kinds of paper, crayons, markers, pastels, play dough.

Include pages from an adult coloring book for those who are not comfortable creating their own artwork.

Have construction paper strips already cut out. Invite reluctant artists to make a paper chain, like the ones children make for a Christmas tree, and write messages about a special place on the strips of the chain.

- Consider expressing your place in a hands-on project.

- Consider a "before and after, with and without your loved one" art piece.

Encourage participants to take home art projects to complete.

PLAY: Play soft music while the participants work on their projects. Begin with "If I Could Be Where You Are" by Enya.

CONVERSATION: Invite participants to share their creations and explain how they relate to their special place, their loved one, and their grief.

Closing Reflection

From *A Grief Observed* (C.S. LEWIS)

> I thought I could describe a state; make a map of sorrow. Sorrow, however, turns out to be not a state but a process.... Grief is like a long valley, a winding valley, where any bend may reveal a totally new landscape.

Preserve Your Memories

Preserve our loved one's honest story to share with others.

In this session we will:

- ■ Evaluate, preserve, and share the memories of our loved ones for the next generation.

- ■ Understand grief stages and long-term effects on our well-being.

Welcome and Review

In the previous session, we explored the power of place in our grieving and learned about healthy habits for coping with grief.

In this session, we will determine which memories to preserve.

Activity   Purse or backpack, paper lunch bags, slips of paper

Handout with "What's in your bag?" questions. (See Template.)

Video   *NCIS: "The First Day"*
(February 9, 2021, Season 18, Episode 7),
36:50–39:31 and 41:10–42:40
Or YouTube: "Gibbs and Jimmy talk about Breena"
(18X7) (2:38) and "Torres and Bishop" (18X7 6/6) (1:30)

NCIS: "Winter Chill"
(March 10, 2021, Season 18, Episode 9), 37:26–42:52 or
YouTube: "Fornell's daughter dies of overdose" (18X9)
(Stop at 3:50)

Music   "Bookends Theme: Preserve Your Memories"
from *Bookends* by Simon & Garfunkel

"Somewhere in My Memory" from Home Alone
(music by John Williams, lyrics by Leslie Bricusse)

"I Will Remember You" (music by Séamus Egan,
lyrics David Merenda, and Sarah McLachlan)

Do not let loyalty and faithfulness forsake you;
bind them round your neck,
write them on the tablet of your heart.
[PROVERBS 3:3]

Meditation

For our meditation, we will hear and reflect on two songs about memories followed by a reading that explores the special things we carry with us to remind us of those we love.

PLAY: Simon and Garfunkel, "Preserve Your Memories" from *Bookends*

PLAY: "Somewhere in My Memory" from *Home Alone*

Read

In his collection of short stories of soldiers in Vietnam, *The Things They Carried*, Tim O'Brien describes the items that infantry soldiers were willing to "hump"—carry— with them through the jungle.

The things they carried were largely determined by necessity. Among the necessities or near-necessities were P-38 can openers, pocketknives, heat tabs, wristwatches, dog tags, mosquito repellent, chewing gum, candy, cigarettes, salt tablets, packets of Kool-Aid, lighters, matches, sewing kits, Military Payment Certificates, C rations, and two or three canteens of water. Together, these items weighed between 15 and 20 pounds....They all carried steel helmets that weighed 5 pounds.... Because the land was mined and booby-trapped, it was SOP for each man to carry a steel-centered, nylon-covered flak jacket, which weighed 6.7 pounds, but which on hot days seemed much heavier.... Because the nights were cold, and because the monsoons were wet, each carried a green plastic poncho that could be used as a raincoat or groundsheet or makeshift tent. With its quilted liner, the poncho weighed almost two pounds but it was worth every ounce.... Almost everyone carried photographs.

There were other things they carried that were less necessary.

On ambush, or other night missions, they carried peculiar little odds and ends. Kiowa always took along his New Testament and a pair of moccasins for silence.... Lee Strunk carried his slingshot; ammo, he claimed, would never be a problem. Rat Kiley carried brandy and M&Ms candy....

Henry Dobbins carried his girl-friend's pantyhose wrapped around his neck as a comforter. They all carried ghosts.

CONVERSATION: Simon and Garfunkel exhort us to "preserve your memories, they're all that's left you." John Williams' song celebrates the memory of an ideal Christmas: decorations, lights, gingerbread. Tim O'Brien enumerates the objects that soldiers carried, some that reminded them of home.

- Do any of these pieces resonate with you?

- Do you have a special memory of being with your loved one?

LEARN

Memories and Traumatic Death

"Somewhere in My Memory" represents the idealized version of our memories. The perfect Christmas, for example. But it doesn't work like that. Not all our memories are perfect. Not all deaths are perfect. Some deaths are traumatic. Part of the grieving process is coming to terms with the unhappy memories and the unresolved rifts. Truth telling is the difficult piece of preserving memories. Uncle Fred's alcoholism tore his family apart, or Aunt Sally's suicide devastated her children. However, Fred took in his sister's children when she was undergoing cancer treatment, and Sally took care of her disabled mother.

How do we deal with the reality of a traumatic death, and how do we curate our memories of the loved one in the face of that person's tragic death? (See "Coping with Grief and Loss" handout.)

CONVERSATION: Allow participants to share examples or experiences with public and private trauma and truth.

More Information on Grief:
See "Coping with Grief and Loss" handout.

5. *Grief has no timeline.*
4. *Grief has no prescribed stages. Grief is an ongoing process.*
11. *Grief may be the result of both trauma and loss.*
13. *Grief denied or repressed will emerge eventually.*
10. *Grief requires resilience and coping skills.*

REFLECT

The following short clips illustrate many of the points about grief and loss we have discussed. In the first two clips, Jimmy's wife, Breena, died of COVID-19, and he is struggling to cope. Gibbs' wife and daughter were killed decades earlier; he, too, is still trying to cope.

Colleagues create a memorial service for Breena.

In the third (optional) clip, colleague Fornell's daughter, a recovering addict, dies of a drug overdose, and the NCIS team reflects on loss. The poem read is "Epitaph" by Merrit Malloy.

SHOW: Clips from *NCIS*

CONVERSATION: What do we see in these clips about the stages of grief, duration of grieving, expressing sadness, sharing memories, makeshift memorials, traumatic death, and the support of friends?

- Can you see some of our grief statements in this clip?

- How do you respond to the poem "Epitaph"?

APPLY

What Memories Do You Wish to Preserve?

Think of those credit card commercials that ask, "What's in your wallet?" Grief inspires us to pack a duffle bag, backpack, or maybe a Vera Bradley bag full of memories. We label the imaginary bag with the name of our loved one. We carry it with us because it is packed with the memories we hold dear.

Activity

Have a purse or backpack ready containing slips of paper with the questions, listed in the Templates, which you will pull out one by one and read aloud.

Give each person a lunch bag, slips of paper to write on, and the list of Template questions. Allow a few minutes for discernment and writing.

PLAY: Play background music beginning with Sarah McLachlan, "I Will Remember You."

CONVERSATION: Invite participants to share what they wrote and why.

Closing Thought

Excerpted from "When Great Trees Fall"
(MAYA ANGELOU)

> When great trees fall
> in forests,
> small things recoil into silence,
> their senses
> eroded beyond fear....
>
> And when great souls die,
> after a period peace blooms,
> slowly and always
> irregularly. Spaces fill
> with a kind of
> soothing electric vibration.
> Our senses, restored, never
> to be the same, whisper to us.
> They existed. They existed.
> We can be. Be and be
> better. For they existed.

READ: You may wish to access "The Sounds That Still Echo From 9/11," Peggy Noonan's column on the fifth anniversary of 9/11, published in the *Wall Street Journal* on September 9, 2006 (https://www.wsj.com/articles/SB115774704992357920). It has come to be called "I Just Called to Say I Love You":

> These were people saying, essentially, *In spite of my imminent death, my thoughts are on you, and on love....*
>
> This is what I get from the last messages. People are often stronger than they know, bigger, more gallant than they'd guess. And this: We're all lucky to be here today and able to say what deserves saying and if you say it a lot, it won't make it common or so unheard, but known and absorbed.

In our final session, we will summarize what we have learned and shared about our grief and our lives.

Plan Your Future

GOAL

Gather all the elements of the program to determine where you will take your story and who you will become.

In this session we will:

- Review the elements we have learned about grief, loss, story, and hope.

- Gather our new insights to begin to rewrite our stories without our loved one.

- Use a labyrinth to reflect on what participants have discovered about themselves and their grief while discerning how to plan their future.

MATERIALS

Activity	Reproduction of Chartres labyrinth on card stock. (See Templates.)
	A small, smooth stone.
	Evaluation sheet. (See Templates.)
	Handout on Grief and Loss. (See Templates.)
Video	*Lewis* (from PBS Inspector Lewis series) "The Soul of Genius," Season 6, Episode 1, 1:01:26–1:04:46
Music	**"One More Day"** from Veronica Guerin, by Harry Gregson-Williams, Trevor Horn, Hugh Marsh, and Patrick Cassidy

Welcome and Review of Seven Prior Sessions

Begin by taking a quick look at each of the prior sessions:

SESSION 1: We met your loved one and learned about your loss.

SESSION 2: We met you and learned about your story.

SESSION 3: We explored the conflicting forces of holding on and letting go.

SESSION 4: We explored the power of music to express our grief and help us heal.

SESSION 5: We explored the power of the visual arts to lead us to hope.

SESSION 6: We used the power of place to learn more about healthy responses.

SESSION 7: We found ways to preserve our memories of our loved ones.

In this session – We pull it all together and examine "who we will become" as we write our new chapters.

Meditation

What is our goal as we wrap up the program?

...my soul is bereft of peace;
*   I have forgotten what happiness is;*
so I say, "Gone is my glory,
*   and all that I had hoped for from*
*   the Lord."*

The thought of my affliction and
my homelessness
*   is wormwood and gall!*
My soul continually thinks of it
*   and is bowed down within me.*
But this I call to mind,
*   and therefore I have hope:*

The steadfast love of the Lord never ceases,
*   his mercies never come to an end;*
they are new every morning;
*   great is your faithfulness.*
"The Lord is my portion," says my soul,
*   "therefore I will hope in him."*
[Lamentations 3:17–24]

As we begin to write the new chapters for our lives, can we go from:

> *...my soul is bereft of peace;*
> *   I have forgotten what*
> *happiness is;*

to:

> The steadfast love of the Lord
>   never ceases,
>   his mercies never come
>   to an end;
> they are new every morning?

Read: "Fifteen Years after a Fatal Crash" by Thomas Farragher, published in *The Boston Globe* on April 6, 2016 (https://www.bostonglobe

.com/metro/2016/04/05/remembering-oak-hill-bus-crash-years-later/RNdrCPNKFIXdiQaTJLhNCN/story.html).

She was a carefree teenager sitting in the back of a bus bound for a springtime weekend of soaring music in Nova Scotia.

One moment, Kayla Rosenberg and her pals from a Newton middle school were quietly singing "Bohemian Rhapsody," the Queen rock anthem. And then, 350 miles from home and in the darkness just before dawn, the bus driver missed his exit and flipped over on a hairpin turn in New Brunswick.

Kayla and three other students... were killed and dozens were injured in an accident that was an emotional earthquake that tore through a close-knit school.

...Through the years, Donna Rosenberg has kept her last conversation with her thirteen-year-old daughter close to her heart—words forever preserved in a kind of spiritual locket.

..."She said, Mommy, I'm so happy I went on this trip. I'm having the best time. I'm really happy....And she said three times, 'Mommy, I love you.' And I said to her: 'Kayla, I love you more than life.'"

Within hours, Kayla, along with [her three classmates]—all sitting in the rear of the bus where a window popped open—were dead.

"There's nothing worse than losing a child," Donna Rosenberg told me...."It's hard work. It's hard work every day."

For a while she could not write Kayla's name. She could not write her address. "The bottom fell out," she said. She sought help and got it from a social worker who helped her climb out of the darkness.

Like the families of the other kids who were killed, the Rosenbergs...have found ways to memorialize Kayla. Their survivors have established funds to do good work in the names of the students who left on a musical adventure and never came home. Help for the sick and the homeless and the hungry.

...Within hours after the crash, fifty of Kayla's friends arrived at the Rosenberg home to offer comfort. Kayla's mom had a request. She wanted to take their picture. She wanted to remember them. And she wanted them to remember Kayla.

"I asked them to open their hearts to let whatever spirit of my child was left into their heart so that she would have a safe place to be," she said then. "I asked them to remember her to their children. And when they had children to use her as a story to pass on about this wonderful girl they knew when they were in middle school."

Some of those kids are married now. For a while, Donna Rosenberg kept in touch. [But now] "I felt it's time to let them go," she said. "It's time to move on. They need to stop grieving. They need to be happy."

Like anyone who's lost a child, the Rosenbergs know how difficult that journey is—an everlasting work in progress.

CONVERSATION: Given everything we have learned, what do you see and hear in the Rosenbergs' story? About trauma, grieving, memories, holding on, and letting go?

LEARN

See "Coping with Grief and Loss" handout. Why is grieving necessary?

1. *Grief helps us find a new reality.*

REFLECT

SHOW: *Lewis* clip
Inspector Lewis, speaking from his own experience with the loss of his wife, reminds a grieving mother that eventually her memories of her son should be less about his death and more about his life.

CONVERSATION: Can you evolve from memories of death to memories of life? What is your response to the advice from Lewis about acceptance, about not reliving the death, and that eventually memories should be more about the life of a loved one and less about that person's death?

APPLY

Activity

Handout: Chartres Labyrinth, stones, and questions from Templates.

We will use a labyrinth to review what we have learned and to think about three questions:

- Who was I with my loved one?
- Who am I now?
- Who will I become without my loved one?

Explain that a labyrinth:

- Is not a maze, a puzzle, or a trick.
- Is a series of concentric circles with no dead ends.
- Is one continuous walking path from the outer edge to the center. One can always turn to see the center and turn to see the entrance/exit.
- Is designed with twists and turns and double backs, just like life.
- Is a tool: a pathway for meditation and reflection.
- Can be found in medieval cathedrals, retreat centers, college campuses, and memorial gardens.

- Could be the visual representation of the questions Who was I? Who am I? Who might I become?

Walk the Labyrinth

Give participants time to "walk" the labyrinth and answer the questions.

PLAY: "One More Day," the funeral song from the movie *Veronica Guerin*, while participants work on their labyrinths.

- Walking into the labyrinth answers the question: Who was I?
- Standing at the center answers the question: Who am I?
- Walking back out answers the question: Who will I become?

As persons of faith, we know we are never alone on our labyrinth journey.

> *But now, thus says the Lord...*
> *Do not fear, for I have redeemed you;*
>   *I have called you by name, you*
> *are mine.*
> *When you pass through the waters, I*
> *will be with you;*
>   *and through the rivers, they shall*
> *not overwhelm you;*
>   *when you walk through fire you*
> *shall not be burned,*
>   *and the flame shall not*
> *consume you.*
> *For I am the Lord your God...*
> *you are precious in my sight,*
>   *and honored, and I love you...*
> *Do not fear, for I am with you...*
> [Isaiah 43:1–5]

CONVERSATION: Invite participants to reflect on their labyrinth journey.

Participants' Review

Give participants time to fill out the evaluation sheets found in the Templates at this point or when the session is completed.

Grief and Loss Handout

Distribute the "Coping with Grief and Loss" handout from the Templates.

Closing

Take the hearts down from the Remembrance Board before the session begins and arrange them around the candle. Invite participants to retrieve their hearts.

READ TOGETHER: John Henry Cardinal Newman

> O Lord, support us all the day long,
> until the shadows lengthen, and the
> evening comes,
> and the busy world is hushed,
> and the fever of life is over,
> and our work is done.
> Then in your mercy,
> grant us a safe lodging,
> and a holy rest,
> and peace at the last.

Each of you is on your own road. You are alone on that road. Stop and look back. What do you see?
   Now, turn and look forward.
What do you want to see?
   Start walking.

Collect Evaluations and Thank Yous

BIBLIOGRAPHY

Angelou, Maya. *I Shall Not Be Moved*. New York: Penguin Random House, 1990.

Bonhoeffer, Dietrich. *A Year with Dietrich Bonhoeffer: Daily Meditations from His Letters, Writings, and Sermons*. Edited by Carla Barnhill. New York: Harper Collins, 2005.

Cacciatore, Joanne. *Bearing the Unbearable: Love, Loss and the Heartbreaking Path of Grief*. New York: Wisdom Publications, Simon and Schuster, 2017.

DeLeon, Roy, ObiSB. *Praying with the Body: Bringing the Psalms to Life*. Brewster, MA: Paraclete Press, 2011.

du Maurier, Daphne. *Rebecca*. New York: Avon Books, 1971.

Farragher, Thomas. "Fifteen Years after a Fatal Crash." *Boston Globe,* April 6, 2016.

Hackenberg, Rachel G. *Writing to God: 40 Days of Praying with My Pen*. Brewster, MA: Paraclete Press, 2011.

Keenan, James F., SJ. *Ethics of the Word: Voices in the Catholic Church Today*. New York: Rowman and Littlefield, 2010.

Keenan, James F., SJ. *Virtues for Ordinary Christians*. New York: Rowman and Littlefield, 1996.

Kelley, Melissa M. *Grief: Contemporary Theory and the Practice of Ministry*. Minneapolis: Fortress Press, 2010.

Kübler-Ross, Elisabeth. *On Death and Dying*. New York: Macmillan, 1972.

Kübler-Ross, Elisabeth, and David Kessler. *On Grief and Grieving*. New York: Scribner, 2014.

The Labyrinth Society. https://labyrinthsociety.org/resources.

Lennan, Richard, and Nancy Pineda-Madrid, eds. *Hope: Promise, Possibility, and Fulfillment*. Mahwah, NJ: Paulist Press, 2013.

Lewis, C.S. *A Grief Observed*. New York: Harper Collins, 1996.

Long, Thomas G. *Accompany Them with Singing: The Christian Funeral*. Louisville, KY: John Knox Press, 2009.

MacIntyre, Alasdair. *After Virtue: A Study in Moral Theory*. Notre Dame, IN: University of Notre Dame Press, 2007.

Meeks, Wayne, general ed. *The Harper Collins Study Bible: New Revised Standard Edition*. New York: Harper Collins, 1993.

Noonan, Peggy. "The Sounds That Still Echo from 9/11." *Wall Street Journal*, September 9, 2006.

O'Brien, Tim. *The Things They Carried*. New York: Penguin, 1991.

O'Donohue, John. *To Bless the Space Between Us*. New York: Convergent Books, 2008.

Oliver, Mary. *Thirst*. Boston: Beacon Press, 2007.

Penny, Louise. *A World of Curiosities*. New York: Minotaur Books, 2022.

Rambo, Shelly. *Spirit and Trauma: A Theology of Remaining*. Louisville, KY: Westminster John Knox Press, 2010.

Rupp, Joyce. *May I Have This Dance*? Notre Dame, IN: Ave Maria Press, 2007.

Sloyan, Virginia, ed. *Death: A Sourcebook about Christian Death*. Chicago: Liturgical Training Publications, 1989.

Valentin, Benjamin. "Theological Writing and the Power of Place." Continuing Education Lecture, Boston College School of Theology and Ministry, Chestnut Hill, MA, November 10, 2022.

Van Der Kolk, Bessel. *The Body Keeps the Score: Brain, Mind, and Body in the Healing of Trauma*. New York: Penguin, 2015.

Van Deusen Hunsinger, Deborah. *Bearing the Unbearable: Trauma, Gospel, and Pastoral Care*. Grand Rapids, MI: Eerdmans, 2015.

Templates

He said to them, "Come away to a deserted place all by yourselves and rest a while." MARK 6:31

He said to them, "Come away to a deserted place all by yourselves and rest a while." MARK 6:31

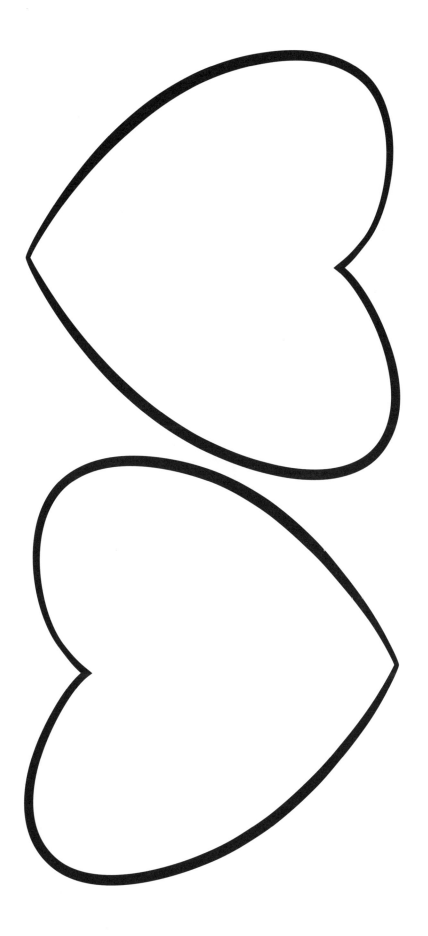

The Empty Bench Meditation

What do you remember about your loved one?

That person's smile or voice? A gesture?
A favorite expression?

**Perhaps you think about what made
that person special to you.**

*What if you placed a bench in your garden or local
park to remember your loved one?*

*If you had to inscribe one word, one phrase, or one sentence on
a brass plate for your loved one's bench, what would it be?*

Think of your special bond with your loved one.

Who Are You?

Fill in the statements that apply to you.

I am the parent of: _____

I am the sibling of: _____

I am the spouse/partner of: _____

I am the child of: _____

I am the grandchild of: _____

I am the cousin, niece, or nephew of: _____

I am the neighbor, classmate, or friend of: _____

The answer to *Who are you?* is your story.

Writing My New Story

Can you define yourself/your story today: *Who are you?*

How will you determine *who you will become?*

Do you need a different theme?

A new plot? A different setting? New characters?

Part of the work of grieving is the struggle to make sense of what has happened by reconstructing our story. Were you handed a "box full of darkness"? Can you find the "gift"?

MAJOR move pet children AWAY PERMANENT without friend death ALSO LOSS future purpose selling. chronic isolated illness bankruptcy anxiety feel melancholy depressed house untethered directionless robbery LONLEY career family divorce makes

Museum Card Questions

Why did you choose this picture? _____

_____

What beckons you into the picture? _____

_____

What feelings does it evoke? _____

_____

What associations, memories, and longings
does the picture trigger? _____

_____

Does it remind you of your grief? How? _____

_____

Does it remind you of a particular time, place,
or activity with your loved one? What? _____

_____

What is revealed to you through this picture?
To what, if any, action does it move you? _____

_____

Your Special Place

Can you remember a detail of your childhood bedroom or a favorite play space?

_____

Do you remember something from your grandmother's kitchen or a favorite relative's house?

_____

Describe a memory from your elementary school, high school gym, or college dorm.

_____

Where was the last place you visited with your loved one?

_____

Where is a special place you shared with your loved one?

_____

Can you picture yourself there with your loved one?

_____

What do you find there?

_____

How does it give you comfort?

_____

How do you feel if you have to leave that place?

_____

What's in Your Bag?

Write responses to these questions on slips of paper and pack them in your memory bag. Write as many responses as you wish on separate slips of paper. Throw away the slips with those memories you wish to leave behind.

Which memories of your loved one will you choose to pack in your bag?

Which memories of your loved one will you choose to leave behind?

When will you open the bag?

Will you keep adding to the bag as time passes?

Will you share the contents of the bag with others?

If so, with whom?

Walk the Labyrinth

Take the labyrinth card and use the stone to trace
the path from the outside to the center and back out again.

"The past is behind, the future ahead, and the present is the viewpoint from which we relate to both."
[SHELLY RAMBO, *SPIRIT AND TRAUMA*]

Keep in mind the three questions:

- Who were you with your loved one?
- Who are you now?
- Who will you become without your loved one?

Walk into the labyrinth.

- Think about milestones in your life with your loved one: the activities, challenges, victories, joys, and sorrows you shared. Jot them down if you wish.
- Place asterisks at various points on the labyrinth path to represent these milestones.

Pause at the center of the labyrinth.

- Look back at your life with your loved one, knowing that you must continue the journey without that person.
- In the center, rest, regroup, plan the new chapters. You could place the empty bench in the center of the labyrinth.
- Find peace despite your loss. You may pause in the center, but we cannot live in the center.

Walk out of the labyrinth.

- To get out of the labyrinth, you must walk back along the path without your loved one. What will that journey be like? Where are you headed? How will you get there?
- Consider that your loved one still accompanies you through your new journey, your new life, to your new chapters.

As you walk along the labyrinth path:

- Do you better understand the nature of your grief, your triggers, and your memories?
- What are you holding on to?
- What are you letting go of?
- Do you remember a special place, a special song, a special image?
- Where is the new path leading you?
- What do you feel as you walk along?
- Who is guiding you?

Walking into the labyrinth answers the question *Who was I?*

Standing at the center answers the question *Who am I?*

Walking back out answers the question *Who will I become?*

Chartres Labyrinth Drawing from The Labyrinth Society Resources.

Program Evaluation

Please respond honestly to the questions below.

1. Which session or theme resonated with you? Why?

2. Which session or theme did not resonate with you? Why?

3. Which activity / song / meditation / video clip had meaning for you?

4. Which activity / song / meditation / video clip had minimal meaning for you?

5. Did you have enough opportunity to talk or share?
    Did you find that too much time was spent on sharing?

6. Was the information on grief helpful?

7. Is there a theme, question, or activity that you would add?

8. Would you recommend this program to a friend or family member?

Additional comments?

Coping with Grief and Loss

Thus says the LORD:
Stand at the crossroads, and look,
   and ask for the ancient paths,
where the good way lies; and walk in it,
   and find rest for your souls.

[JEREMIAH 6:16]

What Is Grief?

Grief is the work of remembering who we were with our loved one,

knowing who we are now,

and planning who we will become without our loved one.

Why Is Grieving Necessary?

Grieving allows us to process the loss and all its ramifications.

Grieving guides us to find a meaningful place for the loss in our lives.

Grieving helps us to hold on to the happy memories of the loved one.

Grieving encourages us to let go of trauma and negative memories.

Grieving moves us to break the bonds that hold us in one place.

Grieving helps us to evolve.

Grieving encourages us to create a path to a new reality.

Types of Grievers

INTUITIVE GRIEVERS express themselves outwardly, often through emotion and conversation. They willingly express their grieving though sharing stories, crying, or sad music or movies. Intuitive grievers reach out to others.

INSTRUMENTAL GRIEVERS express themselves inwardly, through thoughts and actions. They stoically bury themselves in work, projects, hobbies, or study. Instrumental grievers prefer to be alone.

Many people are some combination of both styles of grieving. While they may tend toward one or the other style, they are a blend of both behaviors.

Fifteen Truths about Grief

1. Grief helps one find a new reality.
The work of grieving is to find a new reality for one's life. Acknowledge the loss, grieve the loss, and strive to find what will become the new life for yourself. It is not an easy task; it will take time. Only you can determine what that new reality will be.

2. Grief is not a pathology.
Grief is not an illness to "get over."
There is no prescription or cure for grief. One does not get over it. One learns how to live with it in a better way each day.

3. Grief is different for everyone.
Every loss is unique and, therefore, everyone's grief is unique. Similar losses are not the same loss. No one truly "knows how you feel."

4. Grief has no prescribed stages.
Elisabeth Kübler-Ross' stage theory is often misunderstood. No one progresses through exact stages of grief in a rigid order over a set amount of time. Everyone's journey is their own.

5. Grief has no timeline.
Grief is an ongoing process.
Grief evolves at its own pace. You will always feel your loss, just not always in the same way. No one must "move on" in a month, six months, a year, five years. Move forward when you are ready.

6. Grief is personal and intimate.
Your response to your loss is personal to you and influenced by your own background. Everyone who has lost a loved one, a house, a job, or physical mobility is not having the same experience.

7. Grief manifests in numerous and varied ways.
Grief is not revealed only in sadness. Grief can manifest in substance abuse, workaholic behavior, irrational fears, withdrawal, depression, or dangerous risk-taking. Grief can also inspire charity, creativity, new hobbies, new friendships, and new adventures.

8. Grief has triggers.
A song on the radio, a favorite food, or holiday rituals can trigger an episode of grief. Grief can overtake you when you least expect it. Look for understanding from those around you.

9. Grief affects your body and your mind.

Give yourself some space and down time, but don't lock yourself in your room. Grief can make you distracted, fuzzy, forgetful, and tired. Make an effort to be positive, eat well, exercise, and get professional help for feelings of acute depression or self-destruction.

10. Grief requires resilience and coping skills.

Suggesting that one immediately bounce back from loss is unreasonable. Patience in allowing yourself to grieve and to understand your loss will foster resilience. Staying active will encourage you to develop skills for coping with the loss.

11. Grief may be the result of both trauma and loss.

Loss may be the result of trauma, or loss may cause trauma. Be aware that trauma untreated can be very destructive: note post-traumatic stress disorder (PTSD) in war veterans or assault victims.

12. Grief does not happen in a vacuum.

Loss occurs while other things are happening in your life, such as illness, work challenges, relocation, marriage or divorce, and new children. Feeling overwhelmed is natural. Asking for help is essential.

13. Grief denied or repressed will emerge eventually.

Be aware of the effect of your loss on your life as you move forward. Rather than repressing and claiming you are "fine," deal with your grief and loss in the present or it will haunt you in the future.

14. Grief can be about places, pets, and relationships.

We understand grieving for the loss of our family, friends, or pets. We sometimes forget that moving out of a long-time home or neighborhood can be a huge loss, as is coping with retirement, illness, loss of independence, or loss of familiar support systems.

15. Grief requires meaning making.

Loss can initially be unfathomable. Part of the healing process is being able to step back, look at how the loss occurred and why, and determine how one's life will move forward in light of the loss. Grief is about processing and making sense out of what has happened.

STAYING HEALTHY WHILE GRIEVING

- Find a good routine for eating, sleeping, and daily activities.

- Replace unhealthy, addictive behavior with healthy activities.

- Try a new sport, hobby, or travel destination.

- Find good coping strategies, such as talking to a trusted friend or avoiding angry family members and stressful situations.

- Carve out time and space for yourself and your grief.

- Consider counseling. Accept help.

- Be honest. It's OK to say, "I'm not doing so well today."

- Find resources online, at the library, or from healthcare providers on coping with grief.

- Maintain balance in your life, relationships, and activities.

Dealing with Traumatic Death

Name the truth. Loved ones can die from alcoholism, drug overdose, violence, abuse, accident, suicide, or stillbirth. It is a reality we must acknowledge and accept.

Avoid denial. The reality doesn't disappear if we deny what really happened to our loved one. Denial hurts us and can lead to PTSD.

Public information versus private truth. No one but those directly involved has a right to know any information. Share only what you feel comfortable sharing when you are ready to share. Some families use their loved one's traumatic death to help others, while many families wish to keep the circumstances of the death private.

Let go of feelings of guilt, responsibility, regret, and anger. We can feel responsible or angry when a loved one dies in traumatic circumstances. Remember, it is not our fault.

Acknowledge all the memories but hold on to the positive ones. Acknowledge the difficult memories but let go of them. The person was no less loved because their death was traumatic.

Seek professional help. Find a professional who can help you work through the situation of the death and your feelings about it. Counseling can be critical to healing.

"Come away to a deserted place all by yourselves and rest a while."

[MARK 6:31]

MORE **GRIEF MINISTRY** RESOURCES

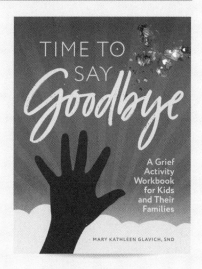

A Parish Guide for Bereavement Ministry and Funeral Planning

JILL MARIA MURDY

The death of a loved one is a shock, and planning a funeral can feel like a burden in a time of stress and grief. Created for pastoral ministers, deacons, pastors, and parish leaders, this booklet is a helpful resource to pastorally accompany Catholic funeral planning—either in advance or after the death of a loved one.

128 PAGES | $16.95 | 6" X 9"
ORDER 853927 | 9781627853927

Reflections and Prayers after the Loss of a Spouse

VIRGINIA STILLWELL

This comforting booklet is specifically for people dealing with the unique grief of losing a spouse. Here, Virginia Stillwell shares consoling prayers, reflections, and psalms to help ease the heavy weight of grief. A wonderful resource for pastoral ministers and anyone involved in parish grief ministry.

32 PAGES | $3.95 | 4" X 6"
ORDER 856799 | 9781627856799

Time to Say Goodbye
A Grief Activity Workbook for Kids and Their Families

KATHLEEN GLAVICH, SND

This gentle, honest workbook is for children ages 6 to 9 who have lost a loved one. Rooted in the hope of Christ's resurrection, it presents the mystery of death and its rituals in ways children can grasp. Includes hands-on activities to help children work through their emotions, and thoughtful suggestions for parents and caregivers.

16 PAGES | $3.95 | 8.5" X 11"
ORDER 856041 | 9781627856041